Ron Vredeveld

THE WAY OF SALVATION

THE WAY OF SALVATION

by GORDON H. GIROD

BAKER BOOK HOUSE
Grand Rapids 6, Michigan
1960

COPYRIGHT, 1960, BY BAKER BOOK HOUSE

Library of Congress Catalog Card Number: 60-53167

PHOTOLITHOPRINTED BY CUSHING - MALLOY, INC.
ANN ARBOR, MICHIGAN, UNITED STATES OF AMERICA
1960

Contents

INTRODUCTION 7

1. ELECTION: ORDAINED TO ETERNAL LIFE 15
2. EXTERNAL CALLING: PREACHING THE GOSPEL ... 29
3. MYSTICAL UNION: LIKE HUSBANDS AND WIVES ... 43
4. REGENERATION: A RESURRECTION
   FROM THE DEAD 57
5. INTERNAL CALLING: GOD OPENS THE HEART 71
6. CONVERSION: REPENTANCE AND FAITH 87
7. FAITH: GIVEN AND REQUIRED BY GOD 103
8. JUSTIFICATION: FORGIVENESS
   AND IMPUTATION 117
9. SANTIFICATION: MORTIFICATION AND NURTURE .. 131
10. GLORIFICATION: COMPLETE REDEMPTION 145

Introduction

The subjects set forth in the chapters of this book together comprise the historic *Ordo Salutis*. The Latin title is commonly translated into the English as the *Order of Salvation* or the *Way of Salvation*.

The *order* which follows is based upon certain presuppositions. The first is the sovereignty of God. As the Scriptures declare, "The Lord, He is God" (I Kings 8:60). Again, "Our God is in the heavens; He hath done whatsoever He hath pleased" (Ps. 115:3). "Known unto God are all his works from the beginning of the world" (Acts 15:18). "In [Christ] . . . we have obtained an inheritance, being predestinated according to the purpose of Him who worketh all things after the counsel of his own will" (Eph. 1:11).

Note the progression of thought in these texts. Not only is God set forth as sovereign, but as One who actively exercises his sovereignty, and specifically in the area of the salvation of man. God has not denuded Himself of his sovereignty in any area or sphere. He has imposed no limitations upon Himself. He is sovereign, and He exercises his sovereignty.

The second presupposition is the total depravity of man in the state of sin. "And you did He make alive, when ye were dead through your trespasses and sins, wherein ye once walked according to the course of this world, according to the prince of the powers of the air, of the spirit that now worketh in the sons of disobedience; among whom we also all once lived in the lusts of our flesh, doing the desires of the flesh and of the mind, and were by nature children of wrath, even as the rest" (Eph. 2:1-3 ASV).

Dead—not ill or disabled—but dead in trespasses and sin. And this state of spiritual death is immediately related to our salvation as a work of God. "But God, being rich in mercy, for his great love wherewith He loved us, even when we were dead through our trespasses, made us alive together with Christ (by grace have ye been saved)" (Eph. 2:4-5 ASV).

The Belgic Confession describes man after the fall thus, "And being thus become wicked, perverse, and corrupt in all his ways, he hath lost all his excellent gifts which he had received from God, and only retained a few remains thereof . . . for all the light which is in us is changed into darkness. . . . Therefore we reject all that is taught repugnant to this, concerning the free will of man, since man is but a slave to sin; and has nothing of himself, unless it is given him from heaven. For who may presume to boast, that he of himself can do any good, since Christ saith, 'No man can come unto Me, except the Father which sent Me, draw him.' Who can speak of his knowledge, since 'the natural man receiveth not the things of the Spirit of God'? In short, who dare suggest any thought, since he knows that 'we are not sufficient of ourselves to think of anything of ourselves, but that our sufficiency is of God'? And therefore what the apostle saith ought justly to be held sure and firm, 'that God worketh in us both to will and to do of his own good pleasure.' For there is no will or understanding, comformable to the divine will and understanding, but what Christ hath wrought in man: which He teaches us, when he saith, 'without Me, ye can do nothing.'" (Art. XIV).

This means, simply, that man is as powerless to help himself in the spiritual realm as is the corpse in the physical. Indeed, the unregenerate man is a spiritual corpse; only by a "resurrection from the dead" can he attain unto life (cf. Ezek. 37:1-14). Upon this is predicated the necessity of regeneration as declared by Christ to Nicodemus, "Ye must be born again" (John 3:7). Thus, too, the *Canons of Dordt* declare, "And this is the regeneration so highly celebrated in Scripture and denominated a new creation; a *resur-*

rection from the dead; a making alive, which God works in us without our aid." (Third and Fourth Heads of Doctrine, Art. XII).

Having accepted these propositions, it follows that man is saved by *grace alone*. He is powerless to bring about his own salvation; he cannot bring himself from death unto life; therefore, his salvation is totally and completely the work of God: "For by grace are ye saved through faith; and that not of yourselves: it is the gift of God: Not of works, lest any man should boast" (Eph. 2:8-9). Note the phrase "and that not of yourselves." Whether the antecedent of "that" be "faith" or the entire clause, "by grace are ye saved through faith," the conclusion must be the same. Salvation is not of ourselves; it is purely of grace, that is, of God and not of man.

As a corollary, we must recognize that "grace" and "works" are mutually exclusive concepts. Paul, speaking of the "remnant according to the election of grace," declares, "And if by grace, then it is no more of works: otherwise grace is no more grace. But if it be of works, then it is no more grace: otherwise work is no more work" (Rom. 11:6). Thus, the Biblical concept of grace does not permit of the notion that man contributes to or participates in his own salvation by any work, act or action, for then it would be "no more of grace."

All this is clearly taught in the Scriptures, in our creedal documents, especially the Canons of the Synod of Dordt, and is deliniated in our earlier work, *The Deeper Faith: An Exposition of the Canons of Dordt*. Now we must take additional steps in understanding the salvation which God provides for us, and the manner in which his salvation is accomplished in our lives.

It is sometimes suggested that the distinctive nature of the Reformed Faith is set forth in the *Canons of Dordt*. Unless this statement receives proper interpretation, it can be misleading. The Synod did not profess to set forth the Reformed Faith in its entirety nor even in all of its distinctive facets. They did set forth five cardinal principles of

Scripture which, if properly and scripturally applied, will lead to a correct understanding of that full-orbed Biblical Faith which we know as Reformed. A fuller deliniation of the Reformed Faith, particularly as it applies to man in the experience of his salvation, will be found in the *Ordo Salutis*.

The *order* in which God accomplishes the salvation of man is set forth in no single verse of Scripture, though an abbreviated *Order of Salvation* may be found in Romans 8:30, " . . . whom He did predestinate, them He also called; and whom He called, them He also justified; and whom He justified, them He also glorified." From this it may be seen that calling, justification and glorification spring from predestination. Indeed, every act and experience pertaining to the redemption of man may rightly be called a fruit of election. Thus the *Canons* declare, " . . . election is the fountain of every saving good; from which proceed faith, holiness, and the other gifts of salvation, and finally eternal life itself, as its fruits and effects, according to . . . the apostle, 'He hath chosen us [not because we were, but] that we should be holy and without blame before Him in love.' Eph. 1:14." (First Head of Doctrine, Art. IX).

From this it may be seen that *election* is the *sine qua non* of salvation. Consider, therefore the classic definition of the *Canons,* "Election is the unchangeable purpose of God, whereby, before the foundation of the world, He hath, out of mere grace, according to the sovereign good pleasure of his own will, chosen, from the whole human race, which had fallen through their own fault, from their primitive state of rectitude, into sin and destruction, a certain number of persons to redemption in Christ, whom He from eternity appointed the Mediator and Head of the elect, and the foundation of salvation." (First Head of Doctrine, Art. VII).

The second link in the "golden chain" of salvation, we have indicated as *"External Calling"* or the preaching of the Gospel. In doing so, we distinguish between "external calling," the preaching of the Gospel, and "internal calling"

INTRODUCTION

in which the Holy Spirit effectually touches the heart of the elect, opening the heart, and causing it to respond to the call of God.

We have suggested "external calling" as the first step within history, and within human experience, because the gospel is to be preached indiscriminately to all men as sinners. Beginning with mystical union and regeneration and continuing through the remaining steps of the *Ordo Salutis,* we shall be discussing the fruits of election as they are wrought in the lives of the elect by the Word and Spirit of God.

The first differentiating step in the life of the elect is *mystical union* with Christ. According to the Apostle John (cf. 15:1-8), man in the state of sin may be likened to a branch cut off from the vine. The severed branch no longer receives life from the vine; it possesses no life in itself; therefore, it is dead. So man is dead, spiritually dead, dead in trespasses and sins. He can no more respond to the preaching of the Gospel than can the physical corpse rise from his coffin. He must be "made . . . alive" (Eph. 2:5 A.S.V.). Then, and not before, is he able to respond to the preaching of the Gospel.

This "making alive" we know as *regeneration,* the impartation of a new life to man. One may argue that union with Christ and regeneration occur simultaneously, but in the divine logic of Scripture, the elect sinner must be ingrafted into the vine, joined to Christ, so that the new life may be imparted to him. The life must flow from the vine to the branch.

Internal or effectual *calling* is closely related to regeneration. The new life must be present, if one is to be able to respond to the preaching of the gospel; yet, the new life does not always respond immediately. Contrary to Arminian opinion, regeneration is not always a cataclysmic or dramatic experience. To use another Biblical figure, the "seed" of the new life may be sown, but it may be some time before it springs up, so that the fact becomes known in the life and experience of the individual. To return to the figure of the vine and the branches, the Holy Spirit must impel or cause the "new man" (the ingrafted branch in whom is the life of the vine) to respond to the preaching of the gospel. Thus we read of Lydia, "whose heart the Lord opened, [so] that she attended unto the things which were spoken of Paul" (Acts 16:14).

The "new man," impelled by the Holy Spirit, makes his response in two ways. He is brought to a conviction of sin, and therefore, he repents of his sin. At the same time he places faith in Christ as the Savior from sin, and more particularly, as *his* Savior. This dual response to the preaching of the gospel, repentance for sin and faith in Christ, we call *conversion*.

Conversion must be distinguished from regeneration. Regeneration is the creation of a new life in man as a result of his ingrafting in Christ. Conversion is the response of the "new man" to the preaching of the gospel. Admittedly, regeneration and conversion may appear to occur simultaneously in some, but the impartation of the new life to the sinner must always precede his repentance and his faith. It is the "new man" who repents of sin; it is the "new man" who possesses faith in Christ as his Savior.

Conversion may be deceptive to the new convert with reference to the place which it occupies in the redemptive sequence. All he knows is that he heard the preaching of the gospel and felt a desire within himself to respond to it; thus, he may assume that only the preaching of the Gospel preceded his conversion. Only a study of Scripture will reveal to him that this is not the case. Because "as many as were ordained to eternal life believed" (Acts 13:48), we know that his faith is the fruit of his election. Because Christ said, "Without me, ye can do nothing" (John 15:5), we know that the branch of his life had been ingrafted into the Vine, who is Christ. Because "it is the Spirit that giveth life . . . no man can come unto Me, except it be given unto him of the Father" (John 6:63, 65), we know that the convert was first born again. Because the "Lord opened" his heart (cf. Acts 16:14), we know that he had received the internal, effectual call of the Word and Spirit. In the sequence which is set forth in Scripture, all these preceded his conversion.

Though *faith* is one of the dual aspects of conversion, it is commonly given individual consideration in the *Ordo Salutis*. This may undoubtedly be attributed to the importance of faith in the life of the redeemed sinner. Calvinism never minimizes faith or the necessity of faith. We must realize, however, that faith is not a work of man but a gift from God. It is an outgrowth of the new nature, impelled by the Holy Spirit. We are vitally aware that "without faith, it is impossible to please God." We must be equally aware that God is the author of our faith through the work of the Holy Spirit (cf. Eph. 2:8-9).

Justification follows faith, for we are "justified by faith" (Rom. 5:1). This in no wise conflicts with the commonly accepted definition of justification as a legal act of God, whereby He declares our sins to be pardoned and imputes to us (puts to our account) the righteousness of Christ. We are indeed justified from eternity, but the experience of justification comes to us only as we possess faith.

Justification is an act of God outside ourselves. *Sanctification* refers to the work of the Holy Spirit within us. In justification, we are declared righteous by God. In sanctification, the Holy Spirit works in our hearts and lives for as long as we dwell upon earth, causing us to "mortify the old man," to eradicate sin from our lives and to replace that sin with a positive righteouseness. The "old man" decreases; the "new man" is nurtured and developed within us. So we grow into the stature of Christ. And so, that which we have in principle, namely, righteousness before God, becomes increasingly a reality in our lives.

Glorification is the final and ultimate step in our redemption; it is the consummation of the work of God in our lives. The last vestiges of the "old man" are removed, and the "new man" is brought to perfection. Thus God brings our redemption to completion through our ultimate glorification.

We enter upon the last stage or step in our redemption only as we experience physical death. Physical death is much more than a separation or departure of the soul from the body. At physical death, the "old man" dies. No longer are we troubled by the old, corrupt nature. It is removed once and forever. And the new nature is perfected, brought to complete fruition.

Thus our redemption is the work of God. The redemptive process began in eternity before the worlds were framed; it concludes in eternity when new men dwell in a new heaven and a new earth. More, the Word and the Spirit must accomplish in us all that God purposed to do from eternity even unto eternity. What shall we say then? To God be all the glory.

"Blessed be the God and Father of our Lord Jesus Christ, who hath blessed us with all spiritual blessings in heavenly places in Christ: According as He hath chosen us in Him before the foundation of the world, that we should be holy and without blemish before Him in love: Having predestinated us unto the adoption of children by Jesus Christ unto Himself, according to the good pleasure of his will, To the praise of the glory of his grace, wherein He hath made us accepted in the beloved" (Eph. 1:3-6 A. S. V.).

1. Election: Ordained to Eternal Life

And when the Gentiles heard this, they were glad, and glorified the word of the Lord: and as many as were ordained to eternal life believed.
—Acts 13:48

Be it known unto you therefore, men and brethren, that through this man is preached unto you the forgiveness of sins:

And by him all that believe are justified from all things, from which ye could not be justified by the law of Moses.

Beware therefore, lest that come upon you, which is spoken of in the prophets;

Behold, ye despisers, and wonder, and perish: for I work a work in your days, a work which ye shall in no wise believe, though a man declare it unto you.

And when the Jews were gone out of the synagogue, the Gentiles besought that these words might be preached to them the next sabbath.

Now when the congregation was broken up, many of the Jews and religious proselytes followed Paul and Barnabas: who, speaking to them, persuaded them to continue in the grace of God.

And the next sabbath day came almost the whole city together to hear the word of God.

But when the Jews saw the multitudes, they were filled with envy, and spake against those things which were spoken by Paul, contradicting and blaspheming.

Then Paul and Barnabas waxed bold, and said, it was necessary that the word of God should first of men, that He had arisen on the third day, and that by his death and resurrection He had wrought redemption.

Surely no one would undertake to suggest that a finer gospel sermon has ever been preached than that one which Paul preached in Pisidian Antioch. The people who heard him that day were gripped by his message. They told others. The next Sabbath, we read, "almost the whole city was gathered together" to hear more from the lips of Paul. This antagonized the leaders of the Jews; they were envious. We read that they "contradicted" Paul and "blasphemed." This led Paul and Barnabas to present their message to the population of the city at large, that is, to the Gentiles who formed the major portion of the city's population. The Gentiles heard Paul's message, and of the number who heard it, some believed; that is, they were converted. They were convicted of their sins and believed on Jesus Christ as their Savior.

Just at this point in the record of the book of Acts, the thirteenth chapter, the forty-eighth verse, a significant statement occurs. This is what we read, ". . . as many as were ordained to eternal life believed." As many as were ordained to eternal life believed! Not one soul more; not one soul less. Here, then, was the elective purpose of God displayed. The gospel was preached. All those who were present heard the Good News of salvation in Christ. Some went on their way in continued unbelief. Some believed. What was the difference between those who believed, and those who refused to believe? One difference, the elective purpose of God. All those whom God had chosen from before the foundation of the world were brought to repentance and faith that day. As many as were ordained to eternal life believed!

Consider the particulars more carefully. First, the gospel was preached in the city. Did all the people of the city hear the preaching of the gospel? The record does not say that. It says, rather, that "almost the whole city was gathered together to hear the word of God." "Almost" clearly is not all; thus, some of the residents of Antioch did not hear the preaching of the gospel. Some were undoubtedly aged and infirm; they could not be present; nor could the ill. In all probability, too, some were very simply disinterested. Thus, some did not hear the gospel message as it was presented by Paul. So it has been throughout the two thousand years since the time of the apostles. Some have not heard the gospel, because it has not been presented to them; others have not heard it, because they have been disinterested in it or indifferent to it. This is why the church has a missionary burden. It is the task of the church to reach the unreached.

At the same time, how will you explain it? How will you explain the fact that in every generation some do not hear the gospel message during the entire course of their lives? From the human point of view, explanation is simple enough. No one came to them with the message, or when they might have heard it, they were prevented by circumstance from hearing it; or again, they would not hear it when they could have. This is the human explanation; but how will you explain it in terms of an omniscient, omnipotent, sovereign God? Will you say that God was helpless, that He was powerless to reach them? Or will you confess that this too lies within the power and authority of God, as He exercises his providential government over the lives of men? There is but one answer for the Christian: that God is upon the throne, that He directs the lives of men and nations, that He brought some to hear the message in Paul's day, just as He does today, and that he permitted some to remain beyond the scope of that message two thousand years ago, just as He does today. If God be God, this is the only answer; there is none other.

Consider a second group. Though some did not hear the message, many did hear the gospel. Out of that group some went away as they had come—untouched, unmoved, unrepentant and without faith in their hearts. Again, so it has always been. How many come into our churches today and go away unbelieving. How many hear the message by means of radio or television and are left untouched by that message.

How many read the gospel message from the printed page and lay the page aside as though they had not read it. So in Paul's day, some came and heard and went away as they had come—unrepentant, unbelieving, still in their sins.

What shall we say of these who go away unbelieving, both in Paul's day and in ours? How will you explain the fact that some who hear the gospel message are untouched by it? Surely this is not due to any defect in the gospel; what calumny this would be, to suggest that the gospel message is defective. The defect lies, therefore, in the person. And what shall we say of that person who is unmoved and untouched by the gospel? There are several inter-related explanations from the human point of view. Some have no sense of sin in their own lives; they have no personal sense of sin and guilt, and therefore, they feel no need of a Savior from sin. The truth of the gospel does not grip their souls. No conviction, whether of sin or of salvation, is born in their hearts.

All this is true, yet it does not reach to the heart of the matter. These things tell us the man has rejected the gospel; one might say they offer an explanation in terms of secondary causes, but they do not probe to man's innermost being to tell us why he has rejected it. The Scriptures do tell us why, clearly and specifically. The Word of God declares that such are "dead in trespasses and sin," just as we all were who have sprung out of Adam. Hear that phrase carefully: Dead in trespasses and sin. The Bible does not say that they are spiritually ill or diseased or impaired—nothing so limited as that; they are dead—in trespasses and sin. The unregenerate man is a spiritual corpse. This spiritual corpse cannot rise and return to life of itself. Only the Holy Spirit of God can bring life to the spiritually dead. In the words of Christ, "It is the Spirit that giveth life; . . . no man can come unto me, except it be given unto him of the Father" (John 6:63, 65 ASV).

This statement of Christ occurs in a significant context in the sixth chapter of John's Gospel. Many people had come in boats to Capernaum to hear Jesus preach. As he

ELECTION: ORDAINED TO ETERNAL LIFE

spoke to them He said, "All that the Father giveth me shall come to me; and him that cometh to me I will in no wise cast out" (John 6:37). You must not separate these two as is so often done. How often have you heard but part of this verse quoted, like so, ". . . him that cometh to me, I will in no wise cast out." How true, but why is the remainder of the verse so seldom quoted, for this is what Jesus actually said, "All that the Father giveth me will come to me; and him that cometh to me I will in no wise cast out." Those who come to Christ, therefore, are those who have been given to Him by the Father. There is neither accident nor chance in the lives of those who come, nor in the lives of those who do not come. Those who come have been given to Him by the Father.

When He spoke these things, some among them murmured. In response to their murmuring Jesus said, "No man can come to me, except the Father which hath sent me draw him . . ." (6:44). Perhaps we do not grasp the import of these words for a moment; nor, apparently, did all the disciples, for we read that they too murmured. When they did, Jesus asked, "Doth this offend you?" (6:61). Then He explained, "It is the Spirit that giveth life; . . . the words that I speak unto you, they are spirit, and they are life. But there are some of you that believe not. . . . Therefore said I unto you, that no man can come unto me, except it were given unto him of the Father" (6:63-65). This is the explanation. The Holy Spirit had not created the new life within them. The old, unregenerate nature reigned within them still. Their murmuring was the reaction of the natural man, in his depravity, to the things of God. This was why they murmured; this was why they had not believed. This is why they walked with Him no more. It is the Spirit which giveth life; the Father had not given the Spirit to these who did not receive his words. The Father had not given the Spirit to these who had not believed; therefore, they would not come, and indeed they could not come; they would not believe, and indeed they could not believe.

Some may be disturbed by this truth; some may find fault with it; some may seek to deny it. Paul anticipated that objections would be raised even as he wrote his Epistle to the Romans; he knew that some who would read his epistle would find fault; thus, we read the words of Paul, "Nay but, O man, who art thou that repliest against God? Shall the thing formed say to Him that formed it, why hast thou made me thus? Hath not the potter power over the clay, of the same lump to make one vessel unto honor, and another unto dishonor" (Rom. 9:20-21).

You see, beloved, we must face this fact squarely in God's Word, however abhorrent it may at first appear to our corrupted human nature and our debased, sinful minds. I say this to you as believers, as children of God. Even as children of God the incapacities of the old nature are still upon us. We do not see all things clearly; quite to the contrary, as the Apostle Paul said, we see "but through a glass darkly." Our vision of spiritual things is distorted; therefore, we must never allow our sin-beclouded minds to impose upon the Word of God. We must accept the Word of God at its face value, not attempting to make the revelation of God conform to our preconceived notions.

What does the Word of God declare? Simply this, that God is sovereign in the matter of salvation, just as He is sovereign in all things. God does have an elective purpose, and He does exercise that elective purpose. They, who will not believe this truth from the Word of God, will not believe it because they do not want to believe it. They seek to rationalize it away. They raise all manner of objections. We had best hear the Word of God as He declares, "Be still, and know that I am God," and in the silence let us hear again his words, "My thoughts are not your thoughts, and my ways are not your ways." We are his possession. The whole human race is his possession. He created the race of men; and even as the potter may do what he will with the clay, so does God have every right to do what He will with his creation, the race of men.

ELECTION: ORDAINED TO ETERNAL LIFE

Now consider a third group. Among those who heard the message from the lips of Paul that day were some who believed. We may safely leave the other two groups behind in our consideration at this point, both those who have not heard the message, and those who heard it and rejected it. We have a great task before us with respect to both of these groups; we have our orders from the Head of the Church. We are to go out into all the world and preach the gospel. Even so, though we give our best effort to this crusade for the redemption of men, still some shall be unreached, and some of those whom we do reach shall not believe. These, I say, we may leave behind in our consideration at the moment; we can do this knowing that God, in his perfect justice and in his perfect mercy, will do what is perfectly right and good.

This is the point at which a great many people stumble in seeking to understand the doctrine of election as it is set forth in the Word of God. They place the emphasis upon the unsaved, rather than upon themselves as believers. Then they profess a great concern for the unsaved; actually, what they are doing is seeking to question God in his dealings with men. This we have no right to do. This is sheer impertinence; worse, it is an abominable form of impertinence. It is a form of spiritual egotism coupled with rationalism. They will not believe that anything can be true which their frail, sin-scarred minds cannot comprehend.

With reference to the unsaved, we need give consideration to but one fact; it is our duty to reach them; it is our duty to present the gospel message to them. We are to do this with all the zeal and fervor at our command. And we are to trust God to bring to salvation whom He will. This is God's business, not ours. We profess to believe that God is perfect in his righteousness, perfect in his justice, perfect in his mercy, and perfect in his love. If we truly believe this, we have neither right nor reason to question the working of God in bringing men to salvation. He will do what is right and good. Since this is true, why would any man seek to question God in his dealings with men? Yet some have the temerity and the impertinence to question the working of God. We had best remind ourselves that salvation belongs unto the Lord and leave the matter in his hands. "Nay but, O man, who art thou that repliest against God?"

It is in relation to ourselves as believers that we need to be concerned about the elective purpose of God. At this point we are concerned with a third group, those who have heard and who have believed. Now we must proceed with extreme caution. Presumably, at least, those of us who are here fall within this third group or category, the category of those who, not only have heard but who have believed. True, some who are present may not have believed unto salvation, and to them we present the message of God's redeeming love in Christ, knowing that the Spirit of God will bring repentance and faith according to the will of God. It is for those of us who have repented of our sins, who have believed in Christ as our Savior from sin, to exercise extreme caution. Why? Unless we do, we shall become spiritual braggarts. Unless we exercise extreme caution in understanding the nature of our salvation, we shall become the victims of spiritual pride.

How Paul sought to prevent spiritual pride in those who were converted through the message he presented! Do you recall his words to the Ephesian Church, "By grace are ye saved through faith; and that not of yourselves: it is the gift of God: Not of works, lest any man should boast" (Eph. 2:8-9). Lest any man should boast; lest any man should fail to accord to God the full glory in his salvation; lest any man should seek to arrogate to himself some merit in his own salvation—lest any man should do this, Paul declares that our faith is the gift of God. Our faith is not our own. Faith is not an inherent possession within man. Nor is faith self-generated within the heart of man. Faith is wrought in the heart of man by the Word and Spirit of God. God creates faith in men. This is the meaning of the Word of God when we read, "As many as were ordained to eternal life believed." God had ordained that they should receive eternal life; therefore, God wrought faith in their hearts.

This is how men came to believe when Paul preached in Pisidian Antioch two thousand years ago. This is how men come to believe today. This is how you came to believe. This is how I came to believe. As many as were ordained unto eternal life believed. And so they shall today; as many as are ordained unto eternal life shall believe, for God will work faith in their hearts by the Holy Spirit.

Jesus stated the same truth when He said, "It is the Spirit that giveth life. . . . No man can come unto me, except it be given him of the Father." To as many as are ordained unto eternal life, the Father sends the Spirit, working that spiritual transformation in the souls of men whereby they are born again into the Kingdom of God.

Permit me to spell it out. Do you know how you came to Christ? Perhaps you are a young convert. All you know is that you came to the church one day; perhaps a friend had invited you to come. You heard the gospel preached. It struck a responsive chord in your soul. You believed. You came before the consistory of the church, and you made confession of your sins not only, but of your faith in the Lord Jesus Christ as the Savior of your soul. Wonderful! But why did you come? How did you come? You say to me, "I came because I wanted to come. I heard and I believed, and I wanted to confess my faith in the Lord Jesus as my Savior." Of course you did, God bless you.

Still, how did that faith come to exist in your heart? The Word of God declares that once you were dead in trespasses and sin, so utterly dead spiritually that Jesus said you could not have come, except the Father which sent Him should draw you to Him. This is why you came; this is why faith came to be born in your heart; the Father, who sent his only begotten Son into the World, reached out and drew you to his Son. How did He do it? He sent the Holy Spirit into your heart, so that the Word and Spirit created a new heart and a new life in you. That is why you must hear the words of Jesus, "It is the Spirit which giveth life. . . . No man can come unto me, except it be given him of the Father."

Do you know what this means? It means that God must be accorded all the glory in your salvation. It means that God took you, a vessel chosen unto honor, but which had fallen into dishonor through sin, and put the Holy Spirit in your heart, so that the Spirit would lead you to Christ, and to faith in Christ, and to redemption through his blood shed upon Calvary's cross. When your faith was new and fresh, when you were but a babe in Christ, you did not realize that this was the case. You may have thought, in your small knowledge of spiritual things, that you had brought yourself to salvation, or you may not have thought about it at all; perhaps you were too happy with your new faith in Christ to ask any questions at all. Now, however, it is time for you to know; it is time for you to mature in the faith; you cannot remain a mere babe forever; you must become a spiritual adult. To do this, you must know the whole truth, that God, and only God, through his Holy Spirit wrought faith and salvation in your heart. It was not an accident; it was not chance that you came to Christ. It was because the sovereign, eternal God, who had chosen you from before the foundation of the world, reached out his own omnipotent hand and drew you to his Son, putting the Spirit in your heart, bringing a conviction of sin and creating faith in Christ as your Savior. You must see it this way as a spiritual adult. Only when you realize that you owe God everything, will you give to Him the glory. Then you will honor Him as we all should; then you will accord to God all the glory in your salvation.

The Westminster Shorter Catechism asks, "What is the chief end of man?" And it answers, "Man's chief end is to glorify God and enjoy Him forever." This we shall do only if we understand our indebtedness to God, and are properly grateful to Him for our redemption. Only if I know how much God has done for me through Christ, will I know that supreme gratefulness which lies at the root of the life which glorifies God. Only if I realize that I owe everything to God, only if I realize that He is the author *and the finisher* of my salvation, only if I realize that all I am and all I have is the gift of his grace, will I possess that deep-seated effervescent, over-flowing sense of gratitude which motivates the life that glorifies God.

And how shall we glorify God? The answer to this question too, along with all others, is to be found only in the Word of God. Hear the words of Christ in his high-priestly prayer, "Father, . . . I glorified thee on the earth, having accomplished the work which thou hast given me to do" (John 17:4 ASV). Ah, there you have it. When we do his work, when we do his will, when we keep his commandments, then we glorify God.

What a task it is; what a humanly impossible task it is! How shall we do it? It is so contrary to the very nature of man. It is possible only by that same grace whereby we were born anew into the Kingdom of God, by that same Spirit who worked conviction and faith in our hearts. It is not possible naturally; it is only possible supernaturally, when God by his Holy Spirit works sanctification and obedience in our hearts. Only one force is strong enough to impel our lives, to move us to do the humanly impossible, and that is the force of the knowledge, born of the Word and Spirit of God, that He and He alone is the author and the finisher of our redemption, that we were hopelessly and helplessly lost, utterly unable to bring about our own redemption, until God in sovereign grace reached out his hand and drew us to his Son by the Holy Spirit—when we realize that God did it all, then we shall glorify God and not before.

2. External Calling: Preaching the Gospel

And he said unto them, Go ye into all the world, and preach the gospel to every creature.
—*Mark 16:15*
For I am with thee, and no man shall set on thee to hurt thee: for I have much people in this city.
—*Acts 18:10*

After these things Paul departed from Athens, and came to Corinth; And found a certain Jew named Aquila, born in Pontus, lately come from Italy, with his wife Priscilla, (because that Claudius had commanded all Jews to depart from Rome,) and came unto them.

And because he was of the same craft, he abode with them, and wrought: (for by their occupation they were tentmakers).

And he reasoned in the synagogue every sabbath, and persuaded the Jews and the Greeks.

And when Silas and Timotheus were come from Macedonia, Paul was pressed in the spirit, and testified to the Jews that Jesus was Christ.

And when they opposed themselves, and blasphemed, he shook his raiment, and saith unto them, Your blood be upon your own heads; I am clean: from henceforth I will go unto the Gentiles.

And he departed thence, and entered into a certain man's house, named Justus, one that worshipped God, whose house joined hard to the synagogue.

And Crispus, the chief ruler of the synagogue, be-

lieved on the Lord with all his house; and many of the Corinthians hearing believed, and were baptized.

Then spake the Lord to Paul in the night by a vision, Be not afraid, but speak, and hold not thy peace:

For I am with thee, and no man shall set on thee to hurt thee: for I have much people in this city.

And he continued there a year and six months, teaching the word of God among them."

—Acts 18:1-11

We want to begin by pointing to the relationship between two passages of Scripture which may, at first glance, appear unrelated to each other. The first is the command of Christ to his disciples, "Go ye out into all the world and preach the gospel unto every creature." The second consists of the words spoken to Paul in a vision in the night in the city of Corinth, when the Lord said to Paul, "Be not afraid, but speak, and hold not thy peace; for I am with thee, and no man shall set upon thee to hurt thee, for I have much people in this city."

In the first instance, instruction is given to all who are disciples of Christ. They are to present the gospel in all the world and to every creature. In the second instance, a man who is engaged in this task is given further instruction and reassurance relating to his task. Paul is told, first, that he is to speak, that is, he is to preach the gospel to the people of Corinth. Second, he is told that he is not to hold his peace, even though pressure is being exerted by the Jewish leaders to silence him. Third, he is not to be afraid, for the Lord to whom he bears witness will be with him. Fourth, no man will set upon Paul to hurt him. Paul was not given this assurance in other cities which he visited; in other places he was beaten, stoned, and imprisoned, but the Lord promises that no man will be permitted to hurt Paul in Corinth. Fifth, God has much people in this city.

Now do you see the relationship between these two passages? The one is general, "Go ye out into all the world and preach the gospel unto every creature." The other is particular. Paul is in a particular place, the city of Corinth. He will preach to a particular people, the people who comprise the population of that city. Though the leaders of the Jews will be infuriated by the preaching of Paul, no man will be permitted to hurt Paul in that city, for the Lord will be with him. Finally, Paul is encouraged with the fore-knowledge that God has many people in the city of Corinth who will be converted by his preaching.

Consider the matter step by step. First, Paul is told in the vision that he is to speak to the people of Corinth, that is, he is to fulfill the command of Christ which we commonly call the "Great Commission." We have previously quoted the Great Commission in part; now hear the whole of it. Jesus said, "Go ye out into all the world and preach the gospel to every creature. He that believeth and is baptized shall be saved, but he that believeth not shall be damned." Thus, even as Christ set forth the Great Commission, He indicated that some would believe and be saved, while others would reject the message of salvation and remain under the condemnation of the justice of God. This is our common observation, too, is it not? Out of all those to whom we preach the gospel, some believe, and some do not.

Perhaps this fact was in the mind of Paul immediately prior to his vision. He had just come from Athens where he had preached his famed sermon on the "Unknown God." His experience in Athens had been a most disappointing one. He had seen little fruit upon his labor. He had come directly from Athens to Corinth. In Corinth he had aroused the opposition and antagonism of the Jewish leaders by preaching that Jesus is the Promised Messiah. Trouble was brewing, as it had for Paul in so many places.

The fact that the Lord spoke to Paul in a vision, encouraging him to continue in Corinth and promising him that he would not be injured, would seem to indicate, at the very least, that Paul was discouraged. He may even have thought in terms of leaving Corinth. Had not the Lord Himself said to his disciples, during the days of his earthly ministry, "And whosoever shall not receive you, nor hear your words, when ye depart out of that house or city, shake off the dust of your feet"? (Matt. 10:14). Paul and Barnabas had literally carried out this injunction at an earlier date in Antioch of Pisidia. They had not shaken off

EXTERNAL CALLING: PREACHING THE GOSPEL   33

the dust of their feet against the entire city of Antioch, for they had won converts there, but when the leaders of the Jews rose up against them, we read that Paul and Barnabas "shook off the dust of their feet against them, and came unto Iconium" (Acts 13:51). It is possible that Paul was considering a similar action in Corinth.

Perhaps this is a good point at which to interject that the followers of Jesus Christ are not expected to become door-mats before the world. We are to fear nothing, not even persecution or death, but we are not to dishonor the Christ whom we represent, nor the message which we present by permitting either Christ or his gospel to be besmirched and befouled by the world. Sooner or later the decision must be made: How often shall we return to the man who refuses to heed our words? The fields are white unto harvest, the time is short and the laborers are few. Pious sentimentalism may dictate that we return again and again, endlessly, to those who spurn the word of the gospel, but a point must come when we "shake the dust from our feet," figuratively if not literally, and be on our way to others who are waiting.

It is a reasonable presumption that this was the thought in the mind of Paul as the conflict began to develop in Corinth; therefore, the Lord spoke to him in a vision in the night saying, "Be not afraid, but speak, and hold not thy peace, for I am with thee, and no man shall set upon thee to hurt thee, for I have much people in this city." Thus, the Lord said to Paul, in effect, I am coming to you now, Paul, to tell you what you could not know. I have much people in this city; therefore, this is not one of those cities where you are to shake the dust from your feet. You are to stay here; you are to preach to the people of this city, and you will see fruit upon your labors, for I have much people in this city.

Take note that Paul could not know this was the case, until it was revealed to him by the Lord in a vision, but the Lord knew. He could tell Paul that among the people of Corinth were some, in this case even many, who would be converted by the preaching of Paul. Why was the Lord able to give Paul this information? Because God had ordained it so from eternity!

This should cause us to perceive immediately that the preaching of the gospel is by no means a haphazard undertaking. We are under the same orders as the disciples of Jesus' day; they are general orders; we are to go out into all the world and preach the gospel. At the same time, we must understand that this is not to be done by chance or happenstance. God is a God of order. He also sees the end from the beginning. His plans for the redemption of men are calculated to the minutest detail. He sends a particular preacher of the gospel to a particular place at a particular time, and He does so, because he has certain particular people in that place, at that time who are to be brought to salvation by the preaching of that man.

Though Paul was entering a new field, the situation was not materially different in this respect than among established churches today. I believe, as does every other minister of the gospel, that I am serving the church which I am, because God intended me to be here. The congregation assents to the same fact. In acting to call a minister as their pastor, they prayerfully seek to determine the will of God in calling the man whom they believe God would have to preach the gospel in their midst. The minister, in accepting their call, corroborates their judgment of spiritual fact; he comes, because he, too, believes that God would have him preach the gospel in that place. One more fact must be added to these however; God has an end in view in leading a congregation to call a particular man; God also has an end in view in sending a man to a particular congregation. Through that particular man, in that particular place, at that particular time, God will bring certain particular people to redemption, and, in an established congregation, He will sanctify the lives of others through the preaching of that man.

The specific character of the situation will be further clarified, if we recall the passage in Acts 13 which relates the

EXTERNAL CALLING: PREACHING THE GOSPEL 35

experience of Paul in Pisidian Antioch. There, too, God sent a particular preacher; the preacher in that instance also was Paul. He sent Paul to a particular place; it was Antioch of Pisidia. Paul preached the gospel to a particular people, the people of that city. And then, as you will recall, we read those decisive words, "As many as were ordained to eternal life believed." (Acts 13:48). Now we understand what God means when he said to Paul concerning Corinth, "I have much people in that city." God had ordained that many of the people of Corinth should receive eternal life. They would be brought to redemption and life through the preaching of Paul, and God revealed this information to Paul beforehand, so that Paul would be encouraged to prosecute his task of preaching the gospel in Corinth.

Actually, God was illustrating in the life and experience of Paul a great principle which Paul was later to set forth in his epistle to the Romans. The principle is simply this, ". . . whom He did predestinate, them He also called; and whom He called, them He also justified: and whom He justified, them He also glorified." (Rom. 8:30). As Paul began his work in Corinth, God said to him, in effect: Paul, I have predestinated many people in this city to eternal life. Through your preaching I will call them to my Son and to salvation in Him. Therefore, Paul, go to work. The results of your labors are assured.

Then God gave Paul a further promise. It was, "I will be with thee, and no man shall set upon thee to harm thee." Do you perceive all that is implied in this promise? Quite clearly, God must exercise control over the lives of all men in order to make this promise possible. What a tremendous promise this was! In that great and wicked city of Corinth, no man shall be permitted to stretch forth his hand to do Paul harm. We must see this for what it is, a clear illustration of the sovereignty of God over the lives of all men.

Two factors are involved here. First, God is able to declare to Paul beforehand that many will be converted through the instrumentality of his preaching; thus, we see the sovereignty of God in salvation. More than this, however, for even as God is bringing men to salvation through the preaching of Paul, God is also exercising his power over the lives of those who will reject Paul's message, and who will rebel against that message, so that they shall not harm Paul. To sum it all up in a single sentence, here we see God exercising his sovereign government over the lives of all men.

Following the vision, Paul remained in the city of Corinth for eighteen months, preaching the gospel to the people of that city. Now take note. God had informed Paul that He had many people in the city of Corinth, but God did not reveal their identity to Paul. God could have, you know. God could have given Paul their names and their addresses, but this is not God's method. There is nothing mechanical in the means which God uses for bringing men to salvation. Neither does God employ methods which violate the nature with which He created man. God uses spiritual means, his Word and his Spirit working jointly together, to accomplish the salvation of man. Therefore, Paul was ordered to preach to all the people of the city without discrimination or selection, so that out of the total number, by his Word and Spirit, God might call to the Savior those whom He had predestined to eternal life.

This preaching of the gospel to all men indiscriminately is known as "external calling." Perhaps we had best spend a moment with each of these words. The term "calling" is a familiar one. We understand it to mean the invitation which God extends to men to be reconciled unto Himself. This invitation appears in many forms, all of them related to and grounded in the death and resurrection of Christ. The prophet Isaiah sets forth the invitation like this, "Come now, and let us reason together, saith the Lord: though your sins be as scarlet, they shall be white as snow; though they be red like crimson, they shall be as wool." (Isa. 1:18). Jesus Himself presented a similar call to reconciliation when He said, "Come unto me, all ye that labor and are heavy laden, and I will give you rest." (Matt. 11:28). Again, in

EXTERNAL CALLING: PREACHING THE GOSPEL

the final chapter of John's Revelation we read, "And the Spirit and the bride say, Come. And let him that heareth say, Come. . . . And whosoever will, let him take the water of life freely." (Rev. 22:17). This is what we mean by "calling;" it is the call or invitation of God to all men to become reconciled to Himself.

Now we must consider the term "external." We have said that the preaching of the gospel is known, not merely as "calling" but as "external calling;" that is, we modify the term "calling" with the qualifying adjective "external." The Merriam-Webster Dictionary defines "external" as "outward, exterior, applied to the outside of the body." This is exactly what we mean when we speak of the preaching of the gospel as "external calling." The message touches the exterior of the man. He hears the call or invitation of God with the ears of the body, but unless he is born again, so that the ear of faith has been restored to him, he cannot hear with his soul.

Have you ever been puzzled by the passage which speaks of those who have ears but who do not hear, who have eyes but do not see, who have hearts but do not understand? (cf. Isa. 6:9-10; Matt. 13:13-15). What can this mean? You must go back to Eden's Garden for the answer. God had warned our first parents that in the day in which they should sin against his commandment, they should die. (cf. Gen. 3:3). They did sin against the commandment, and they did die. Being cut off from God, the spiritual nature of Adam shriveled within him. This has been the condition of man ever since; in the words of Paul, the unregenerate man is "dead in trespasses and sin." Now the ears of a dead man do not hear; the eyes of a dead man do not see; and the heart of a dead man does not understand. Therefore, God must create a new life within man; he must be born again; then he will have the ear of faith to hear the things of God; then he will have the eye of faith with which to behold spiritual things; then he will have a heart which is capable of understanding the spiritual.

All this underlay the message which the Lord gave to Paul in his vision. When God said to Paul, "I have much people in this city," there were but a handful of converts in the city of Corinth. The "much people" of whom God spoke had not yet come to either repentance or faith. Humanly speaking, they were just like all the other people of Corinth. Within them was the same corrupt, depraved nature which is the spiritual affliction of all men. But God had singled them out. Thus the Lord sent Paul to preach in that city, so that by his Word and Spirit, He would infuse new life into those whom he had predestinated unto life eternal. With that new life, being born again, having become new creatures, they would be given ears to hear and eyes to see and hearts to understand. Then they would come to repentance and faith, and thus, they would become the "much people" of whom God spoke.

I am aware that this truth has proved a stumbling block to some. In a Bible class where we were discussing this matter one day, a man asked, "Aren't you forgetting something? If God must enable a man to come to repentance and faith, how can we say that those who reject the message are responsible for their lost estate? This is a *non sequitur*. There is a gap in the reasoning of anyone who comes to this unwarranted conclusion. To say that God is responsible for man's salvation is a very different thing than to say that God is responsible for man's sinful condition. Man alone is responsible for his plight. God did not create man wicked and perverse, as he is today. To the contrary, God created man "good" and "in his own image. . . . In the likeness of God created He him." By an act of deliberate rebellion man brought himself to the place where he is, under guilt and condemnation.

More still, those who are so concerned about the ability of man to exercise his own will are just exactly half right. Man is quite capable of exercising his will to do evil; man is quite capable of exercising his will to reject the salvation of God. Those who reject the gospel and the Christ who stands at the heart of it do so because of the perverseness of their own natures. By an act of their own rebellious will they spurn the offer of salvation. They reject the message of redeeming grace because of the hardness of their own hearts. This is the exercise of the will of man, when he rejects the overtures of divine mercy.

What man is not able to do, in himself, is to bring himself to salvation. Man is quite able to bring himself to condemnation. This he does by the exercise of his own will. What man cannot do is to bring himself to salvation. This God must do for him by creating a new nature within him. This God does in those whom He has chosen to call unto Himself.

It is this latter truth with which we are presently concerned. I wonder, do you grasp the full meaning and implications of this truth? Do you know what it means to every missionary who goes to the field? Do you know what it means to every minister who preaches the gospel from the pulpit of an established congregation? Do you know what it means to every child of God who bears witness to his Lord whenever and wherever he can? It means that the fruits upon our labors are assured. We do not go forth dependent upon the whims of men. When we stand before a group of people with the message of the death and resurrection of Christ, bringing to them the invitation of God, "Come, let us reason together, saith the Lord, though your sins be as scarlet, they shall be as snow; though they be red like crimson, they shall be as wool"—when we present that message, we know that God will use it along with his Spirit, the Word and the Spirit working together, to create a new life in those whom He would have for his own. He will give them the ear of faith and eye of faith and the heart of faith.

We need not stand before men, whining, begging and pleading. We know the old atheistic assertion is totally wrong; man is not "the master of his fate"; man is not "the captain of his soul." Nor is it merely that we are not dependent upon the whims of men; the basic fact is that God is not dependent upon the whims of men. ". . . whom He did predestinate, them He will also call; and whom He calls, them will He also justify; and whom He justifies, them will He also glorify."

Consider that remarkable passage in the first chapter of John's Gospel, though it is so often misinterpreted. In the eleventh and twelfth verses we read, "To as many as received Him, to them gave He power to become the sons of God. Who were born, not of blood, nor of the will of the flesh, nor of the will of man, but of God." (John 1:11-12). Consider this passage for what it really says. To as many as received Him, to them gave He power to become the sons of God. Indeed, but how were they enabled to receive Him? Remember, they were dead in trespasses and sin. They had ears that hear not, eyes that see not, and hearts that did not understand. How, then, could they receive Him? Because they were born again! And how were they born again? Not of blood, nor of the will of the flesh, nor of the will of man, but of God. What a prelude this makes for that powerful statement from the pen of Paul, "So then, it is not of him that willeth, nor of him that runneth, but of God that hath mercy." (Rom. 9:16 ASV).

What a difference this makes, I say, as we go out to preach the gospel. And we must go out, for as Paul asks, "How then shall they call on Him in whom they have not believed? and how shall they believe on Him of whom they have not heard? and how shall they hear without a preacher? And how shall they preach, except they be sent? as it is written, How beautiful are the feet of them that preach the gospel of peace, and bring glad tidings of good things." (Rom. 10:14, 15). Go out we must, but we go knowing that we are dependent, not upon man but upon God. The fruits upon our labors shall come, not from the whim nor the will of men but from the good pleasure of God.

Go, then, yes, everyone of you, and tell all men, all those with whom you come in contact, all those with whom you are associated, tell all men everywhere—tell them that God has sent his only begotten Son into the world, that whosoever believeth on Him shall not perish, but have everlasting life. Did I say, "Whosoever?" Of course I did. This is part and parcel of our message, that whosoever shall call upon the name of the Lord shall be saved. The invitation is extended to all men. The Spirit and the bride say, Come. Whosoever will, let him take of the water of life freely. But know this beloved, as you carry out this great commission from Christ, you are not dependent upon the will or the whim of men. You shall see fruit upon your labor, rather, because this is the good pleasure of God.

3. Mystical Union: Like Husbands and Wives

Husbands, love your wives, even as Christ also loved the church, and gave himself for it.
—Ephesians 5:25

Wives, submit yourselves unto your own husbands, as unto the Lord.

For the husband is the head of the wife, even as Christ is the head of the church: and he is the saviour of the body.

Therefore as the church is subject unto Christ, so let the wives be to their own husbands in every thing,

Husbands, love your wives, even as Christ also loved the church, and gave himself for it;

That he might sanctify and cleanse it with the washing of water by the word,

That he might present it to himself a glorious church, not having spot, or wrinkle, or any such thing; but that it should be holy and without blemish.

So ought men to love their wives as their own bodies. He that loveth his wife loveth himself.

For no man ever yet hated his own flesh; but nourisheth and cherisheth it, even as the Lord the church:

For we are members of his body, of his flesh, and of his bones.

For this cause shall a man leave his father and mother, and shall be joined unto his wife, and they two shall be one flesh.

This is a great mystery: but I speak concerning Christ and the church.

Nevertheless let every one of you in particular so love his wife even as himself; and the wife see that she reverence her husband."

—Ephesians 5:22-33

In the liturgical "Office for the Confirmation of Marriage" we read, "Marriage is an honorable estate, instituted of God in the time of man's innocency, confirmed by the teachings of our Blessed Savior, and compared by Paul to the mystical union which subsists between Christ and His Church." It is to the last of these assertions that we here pay heed. "Marriage . . . is compared by St. Paul to the mystical union which subsists between Christ and His Church."

The Apostle Paul drew this comparison in his Epistle to the Ephesians where one may read, "Wives, submit yourselves unto your own husbands, as unto the Lord. For the husband is the head of the wife, even as Christ is the Head of the Church. . . . Husbands love your wives, even as Christ also loved the Church, and gave Himself for it. . . . So ought men to love their wives as their own bodies. . . . For no man ever yet hated his own flesh, but nourisheth and cherisheth it, even as the Lord [does] the Church; For we are members of his body, of his flesh and of his bones." (Eph. 5:22-32).

Then Paul added this significant statement, "This is a great mystery, but I speak concerning Christ and the Church." Thus we learn, as Paul constructs his analogy between man and wife on the one hand, and between Christ and the Church on the other, his first concern is, not with marriage but with the Church. Paul is merely using marriage for illustrative purposes. He is using the relationship between husband and wife to demonstrate the nature of the relationship between Christ and the Church.

We are concerned with this "Great Mystery" of which Paul speaks, the relationship between Christ and His Church. As we approach this subject, you will understand that we are concerned, not only with the relationship of Christ to that Corporate Body which is called The Church, but also with the relationship between Christ and individual believers within the Corporate Body, and more specifically, His relationship to you and to me.

This is true, because the Church is people, and people are the Church. We must understand that the Church is not, first of all, a building. That is why we do not doff our hats when we pass by the church-building, as do members of the Roman communion. Nor is the Church, first of all, an organization or an institution but an organism. This is why, in the New Testament and in Protestantism today, the emphasis is neither upon buildings nor organization as such. So, in Protestant areas, one does not come upon great cathedrals, lavishly constructed and appointed, but surrounded by the hovels of poverty stricken people. This, of course, is common in Mexico, Spain, Italy, and other areas dominated by Rome. These things speak of a totally different concept of the Church.

The Protestant Church takes the position set forth in the New Testament. In the Bible we learn that the Church is Christ's Body, and that believers, who constitute the Church, are, each and all, members of that Body. As Paul put it in the Ephesians passage, "We are members of his body, of his flesh and of his bones." When, too, we read that Christ purchased the Church with the shedding of his blood, we understand that He went to the death of the cross for each one of the members who comprise the Body of His Church. Since this is the case, when we speak of the relationship between Christ and His Church, we are speaking of that relationship which we enjoy with Christ, both as a Corporate Body and as individual members of that Body.

Now we are asking: What is the nature of that relationship? It may be compared, declares the Apostle Paul, to the relationship between husband and wife. This gives rise to a second question, namely, what is the essential nature of the relationship between husband and wife? To this we must answer that the essential nature of the relationship between husband and wife is spiritual. We are aware, of course, that

MYSTICAL UNION: LIKE HUSBANDS AND WIVES

secular society views the marriage relationship as legal and contractual. One must obtain a permit, that is a license, in order to effect the marriage relationship. When the vows are taken, and they may consist in as little as the single question addressed to each person, "Do you take this woman to be your lawful wedded wife?" and "Do you take this man to be your lawful wedded husband?", the license must be returned to the issuing agency where it becomes part of the permanent records of that agency. Further, this contractual relationship cannot be set aside except by a court of law.

When all this has been observed, however, one has not really touched upon the heart of the matter. This fact is demonstrated in the every day experiences of society. Some married men and some married women, for example, do engage in adulterous practices, in spite of legal prohibitions and social disapproval. On the other hand, some husbands and wives, not only *do no* such thing, but they could not conceive of doing it. Why? Not because of a legal bond, not because of a contractual obligation, but because of a spiritual bond which binds them together more closely than courts or contracts ever could.

Every man and woman who enjoy a true marriage relationship together would surely confess that they do not think in terms of courts or contracts. The bond between them is higher and finer, deeper and stronger, more immediate and more real than that. The relationship between them is such that it permeates the core of their beings. It is not an external tie but an internal bond. They are not only "one flesh," but one mind, one heart, one soul at the core of their beings. They are "no longer two but one...."

This is admittedly a difficult matter to put into words. The bond which unites a man and a woman in true marriage is intangible; one cannot touch it with his finger; one cannot see it with the physical eye; one cannot set it forth as a blue-printed diagram; it is something which one cannot know, until he has experienced it; it is something which one must feel in his heart and in his soul.

Despite its intangibility, it is a very real bond, and the result is a very real union. There are husbands and wives who, in the course of their married lives, have been separated from each other by ten thousand miles, and yet, they could not be untrue to each other. I did not merely say, "They *would* not be untrue to each other;" I said, "They *could* not be untrue to each other." It is an utter impossibility. There is a spiritual bond between them; they are bound together in an unbreakable union. Distance is meaningless; circumstances are irrelevant; rich or poor, in sickness or in health, they are bound together, until "death do them part," with a bond that nought in this world shall ever sever.

The bond between Christ and the believer is just that real. The spiritual union between Christ and the believer is just that real. Distance is meaningless; He has ascended into heaven and is seated at the right hand of the Father, yet He could not be nearer, if He were seated beside us in the pew or walked hand in hand with us along the road of life. Circumstances are irrelevant; whether our lives are touched with poverty or prosperity, whether we enjoy physical health and well being or lie in pain upon a hospital bed, we are joined to Him with a bond which cannot be severed even by death.

One of our hymns "I've Found a Friend," puts it this way:
>From Him who loves me now so well,
What power my soul can sever?
Shall life or death or earth or hell?
No, I am his forever.

For a fuller understanding of this relationship, we must return to the dawn of human history. When God created man, he was joined to God by a spiritual bond. It was a bond formed in love, the love of God for the creature whom He had created, and the love of the creature for his Creator.

Then God, in his infinite goodness, forewarned the man whom He had created, "If thou shalt eat of the fruit of the tree, thou shalt surely die"; that is, if you violate our love, the bond between us will surely be broken. And man did it! He transgressed the probationary command; the creature turned against his Creator, and the spiritual bond between God and man was ruptured.

This is the essential meaning and nature of death. God is life, and God is the source of all life. For as long as man remained joined to God, he took his life from God; he lived. When, however, the bond between God and man was ruptured, man was separated from the source of his life, and he died. You see, man is dependent upon God, not only for all other things but for life itself. When man is separated from God, he is separated from the source of his life; only death remains.

This is the relationship which is restored in Christ. The restoration of the relationship between God and man is referred to in some of the most basic texts of Scripture. We read, for instance, that "God was in Christ reconciling the world unto Himself." The Merriam Webster Dictionary indicates that a suitable synonym for "reconcile" is "reunite." There you have it. God and man are reunited in Christ. The relationship between God and man is restored in Christ. This restored relationship is such that the New Testament further declares that the believer is "hid with Christ in God."

This is the spiritual explanation for the fact that the redeemed man receives everlasting life. Jesus said, "He that believeth in Me, though he were dead, yet shall he live, and he that liveth and believeth in Me shall never die." True, but why is this the case? Because in Christ man is restored to God, and God is the source of life. When the bonds of love are restored, the life of God flows into the soul of man, and man lives forever, even as God lives forever. The relationship which was violated and ruptured in Eden is restored in Christ.

Equally important, from this restored relationship in Christ flows every saving good which man may know. At the heart of the matter lies the restoration of the spiritual bond and therefore, of the love-relationship between God and man. This is the Biblical explanation for every spiritual experience which is related to human redemption.

Nor must we reverse the order or sequence. We do not become united with Christ because of some act or experience relating to our redemption; quite to the contrary; every act and experience relating to our redemption proceeds from and grows out of our union with Christ. The new life, from its initial stage in the new birth to its culmination in the state of glory, all proceeds from our union with Christ.

Surely this is the lesson of the figure in John 15 of the vine and the branches. The branch receives its life from the vine. The branch has no life in itself; it receives life through organic union with the vine. Jesus said it plainly enough, ". . . without me, ye can do nothing." (John 15:5). Ye cannot be born again. Ye cannot repent of your sins. Ye cannot manifest faith. Ye cannot bring forth the fruits of the new life. "Without me, ye can do nothing."

For our fuller understanding, consider the matter of conversion. Because of the restored relationship between God and man, man is led to sorrow and repentance for sin. For as long as a man continues in his so-called "natural state," separated and apart from God, he will not know sorrow or repentance for sin.

You have experienced a similar truth in every day life. There are unloving husbands who care not how much they hurt the wives who love them; there are unloving wives who care not how much they hurt the husbands who love them; there are unloving children who care not how much they hurt the parents who love them. This is due to one fact, the fact that love is absent on their part. When a man truly loves a woman, he would not hurt her under any circumstances, and, if perchance, he should hurt her in any way, however unintentional that hurt might be, he is stricken by the fact that she is hurt; he seeks her forgiveness, and if possible, he moves immediately to repair the hurt which he has caused.

So it is between God and man. For as long as man is in his "natural state," prone to hate God and his neighbor, he cares not how much he offends his God. He is unmoved by his offense against the Divine Majesty. He is no more touched by the fact that he has offended God than is the unloving husband who distresses his wife. More, this is a continuing situation. The unloving husband brings hurt and injury to his wife day after day, week after week, year after year, and he neither knows nor cares. His lack of love renders him totally insensitive to his wife's injury. He not only does not care that he is adding daily to her distress; he does not know; he can neither realize nor conceive of the anguish he is causing her.

So also is the attitude of the unregenerate man toward his God. He does not care that his daily life is an offense in the sight of God; but more still, he does not know; he cannot realize that his life is an offense and an insult to God. This is why he does not repent of his sin. He does not realize that his life is sin, that his life is an offense and an insult to God. All this is changed when a man is restored to the love-relationship with God. When a man loves God, he hates himself when he sins. He comes before God in sorrow and repentance. He seeks the forgiveness of God. He is stricken by what he has done and pleads with God for divine pardon.

Note that two things take place when the love-relationship is restored. First, man becomes aware of the nature of his sin in the sight of God. The unloving husband is insensitive to anything his wife may do or think or feel. The loving husband senses immediately when he has offended or hurt his wife. So the man who loves God is sensitive to the things of God; he knows when his life is an offense in the sight of God. Secondly, he cares. Along with knowing that God is offended, he cares when God is offended, and thus, he seeks the pardon and forgiveness of God for his sin.

When, therefore, you see a man who knows sorrow for his sin—real, true, deep sorrow; when you see a man who comes before God daily in penitence and tears for his sin, you may know that you are looking upon a man who loves God; you are looking upon a man who has been restored to the love-relationship with God. He is in union with Christ. He is bound to Christ in love. And in Christ, he has been restored to God.

Faith is also a product of this restored relationship, when God and man are reunited in Christ. One day I come to the Church and hear the gospel preached. I hear the invitation of Christ, "Come unto me, all ye that labor and are heavy laden, and I will give you rest. . . . Ho, everyone that thirsteth, come ye to the waters of life and drink freely." Suddenly I feel within myself a strange compulsion. I have heard the invitation a hundred, perhaps a thousand times before, but I was unmoved and untouched. I look about me now and discover that others are unmoved and untouched today, just as I used to be. But I am moved; I am touched; I say in my heart; Yea, Lord, I want to come. I want to lay down my burdens and drink of the water of life freely. For the first time in my life, I not only feel my need of Christ, but I also have faith to believe that He can and will help me.

What wrought this faith in my heart? Is faith a manufactured product which I have succeeded in self-generating within my heart? Ah, no, not that. For as long as I am alienated from God, faith will be alien to my nature. Did you know that? Faith is not natural to man in his unregenerate state; faith, on the contrary, is the most un-natural thing in the world; or, perhaps I ought to say, more correctly, faith is supernatural. I am joined to Christ. In Christ I am joined to God. Through the bonds of this restored relationship, faith flows into my life. You see, He is the source of my faith, as well as the object of it. This is why I read in the Bible that "faith . . . is the gift of God." When I am rejoined to God, He sends faith into my heart. (cf. Eph. 2:8-9).

Then, because I have repented of my sins and have placed my faith in Christ as my Redeemer, I recognize a new source of life within myself. It was there before I discovered it; it had to be, but now I have discovered it. Whereas once I was "dead in trespasses and sin," now I am "made alive" unto God in Christ. The Bible declares that I am a "new creature in Christ," and so I am.

Now isn't this interesting? A change has transpired in me which is so fundamental, so basic that the Bible describes it as being "born anew," "born again," and "born from above." How did this come to pass? And what did I have to do with it? To what degree am I responsible for it? Just as much and to the same degree as the new born babe in the hospital nursery is responsible for his own birth. A man and a woman came together; from their union a child was born. The child has no responsibility for his own birth. Nor did I for my spiritual rebirth. The new "me" was born of a union between Christ and my old sinful self. Without his transforming power to re-new my life, it would have been impossible, but the Holy Spirit, the Spirit of God, the Spirit of Christ, flowed into my life and brought forth a new creature in Christ Jesus my Lord.

Even at this point, if I am not more advanced in my Christian thinking than are most who are new to the Christian Faith, I will not realize that Christ has done all this for me. In truth, without desiring to dishonor Him, I may actually think that I have done all this. Most new Christians only know that they have heard the gospel; they found it reasonable and desirable; they found faith kindled in their hearts, and they made confession of their faith in Christ. This is all one needs to know in the beginning, but as one's faith deepens, as one comes to a larger knowledge of Biblical truth, he must learn that all this was possible, because, and only because Christ has drawn him close in the bond of love, in that wondrously mysterious manner which we call "Mystical Union."

Someone who is sincerely concerned may ask, "How can

I know, if I truly possess this remarkable spiritual relationship to Christ? I am not sure that I feel I do. Is this something which can only be felt? Is there no more objective way of ascertaining whether I am joined to Christ in the bonds of eternal life?"

As a matter of fact there is a more objective way in which you can know than by mere feeling. In truth, I would not recommend that you place too much emphasis upon pure feeling. This is another form of heresy, that heresy which would subject every other form of religious truth and experience to pure feeling. The psychological constitution of man being what it is, even a secular psychiatrist would tell you that a man cannot safely rely upon what he may feel. We must have a more objective means for determining the reality of our relationship to Christ.

Here are some of the more objective standards by which you can test yourself. Have you confessed your faith in Christ as your Savior? The man who is joined to Christ in the bonds of love, not only loves his Lord but desires that the whole world shall know of his love for God. Therefore, he comes before God, before Christ, before the church, before the world, before angels in heaven and demons in hell, to declare his love for his Lord.

How deeply are you moved when you sin? Are you disturbed by your sin? Do you feel real pain in your breast when you sin against your Lord? Do you go to your Lord in daily prayer, seeking his forgiveness, because you know you have offended Him by your sin?

Do you enjoy the worship of God? The psalmist said, "I was glad when they said unto me, let us go into the house of our God." Is the worship of God something more than a duty for you? Is the worship of God something more than an obligation for you? Now, let us make no mistake about this; the worship of God is both a duty and an obligation, but for the true Christian it is much more than that; he who loves God finds real and profound pleasure in the worship of God.

Is your life motivated by your gratitude toward God? When you are faced with the question of serving Christ, of working and worshipping with his people, as opposed to engaging in secular pursuits, is that issue resolved for you when the thought floods your soul, "Christ has done so much for me that I must put his Church and his Kingdom first?"

Are you striving daily to grow in the Faith? Jesus Himself used an instructive figure, setting forth the restored relationship which man may have to God in Christ. He said, "I am the vine; ye are the branches. He that abideth in me, and I in him, the same bringeth forth much fruit; for apart from me, ye can do nothing." (John 15:5). Here is another decisive test: Are you bringing forth much fruit? He is the vine. The vine fills the branch with life. The branch, in turn, must bring forth fruit. If He is in you, and you are in Him, by the very nature of the case, you must bring forth fruit. More still, if you are not bringing forth fruit, if the fruits of the Christian life are not evident in you, then you had best begin to question yourself. Are you joined to Him? Are you a branch which has been restored to the vine, or is the branch of your life lying unattached in a state of spiritual death?

O, this is something to ponder deep within your soul. Are you as a branch ingrafted into the vine? Is the Spirit of God flowing into your life? If this be true, where is the transformation which the Spirit brings to every human heart into which He enters? Where are the fruits that grow upon the branch of that life which has been restored to the vine? Hear the solemn word of the Lord, "If a man abide not in Me, he is cast forth as a branch, and is withered; and men gather them, and cast them into the fire, and they are burned." (John 15:6).

Ah but, if the fruits of the Christian life are evident in you, you can be sure that this is possible, because, and only because He is in you, and you are in Him, for He Himself said, "Without me, ye can do nothing." If faith and hope are in your heart, if you love God even as He first loved you, then you can be certain that this is possible, because, and only because He is in you, and you are in Him.

Our pleasure in the things of God and our gratitude toward God are products of the restored relationship which we have to God through Christ. John puts it this way, "We love Him, because He first loved us." This is a two-way street; love always is, isn't it? When we love Him so much that his cause and his kingdom and his Church have first priority in our lives, then we can know beyond any doubt that we have been restored to God in the bonds of that love which is in Christ Jesus our Lord.

4. Regeneration: A Resurrection from the Dead

Jesus answered and said unto him, Verily, verily, I say unto thee, Except a man be born again, he cannot see the kingdom of God.

Nicodemus saith unto him, How can a man be born when he is old? can he enter the second time into his mother's womb, and be born?

Jesus answered, Verily, verily, I say unto thee, Except a man be born of water and of the Spirit, he cannot enter into the kingdom of God.

That which is born of the flesh is flesh; and that which is born of the Spirit is spirit.

Marvel not that I said unto thee, Ye must be born again.

The wind bloweth where it listeth, and thou hearest the sound thereof, but canst not tell whence it cometh, and whither it goeth: so is every one that is born of the Spirit. —*John 3:3-8*

The hand of the Lord was upon me, and carried me out in the spirit of the Lord, and set me down in the midst of the valley which was full of bones,

And caused me to pass by them round about: and, behold, there were very many in the open valley; and, lo, they were very dry.

And he said unto me, Son of man, can these bones live? And I answered, O Lord God, thou knowest.

Again he said unto me, Prophesy upon these bones, and say unto them, O ye dry bones, hear the word of the Lord.

Thus saith the Lord God unto these bones; Behold, I will cause breath to enter into you, and ye shall live:

And I will lay sinews upon you, and will bring up flesh upon you, and cover you with skin, and put breath in you, and ye shall live; and ye shall know that I am the Lord.

So I prophesied as I was commanded: and as I prophesied, there was a noise, and behold a shaking, and the bones came together, bone to his bone.

And when I beheld, lo, the sinews and the flesh came up upon them, and the skin covered them above; but there was no breath in them.

Then said he unto me, Prophesy unto the wind, prophesy, son of man, and say to the wind, Thus saith the Lord God; Come from the four winds, O breath, and breathe upon these slain, that they may live.

So I prophesied as he commanded me, and the breath came into them, and they lived, and stood up upon their feet, an exceeding great army.

Then he said unto me, Son of man, these bones are the whole house of Israel: behold, they say, Our bones are dried, and our hope is lost: we are cut off for our parts.

Therefore prophesy and say unto them, Thus saith the Lord God; Behold, O my people, I will open your graves, and cause you to come up out of your graves, and bring you into the land of Israel.

And ye shall know that I am the Lord, when I have opened your graves, O my people, and brought you up out of your graves,

And shall put my spirit in you, and ye shall live, and I shall place you in your own land: then shall ye know that I the Lord have spoken it, and performed it, saith the Lord. —*Ezekiel 37:1-14*

Most evangelical hymnals contain a hymn which tells something of the story which is related in the third chapter of John's Gospel. The hymn reads like this:

> A ruler once came to Jesus by night,
> To ask Him the way of salvation and life;
> The Master made answer in words true and plain,
> "Ye must be born again."
>
> Ye children of men, attend to the word
> So solemnly uttered by Jesus the Lord;
> And let not this message to you be in vain,
> "Ye must be born again."
>
> O ye who would enter that glorious rest,
> And sing with the ransomed the song of the blest;
> The life everlasting if ye would obtain,
> "Ye must be born again."
>
> A dear one in heaven thy heart yearns to see,
> At the beautiful gate may be watching for thee;
> Then list to the note of this solemn refrain,
> "Ye must be born again."

The ruler who came to Jesus by night was, of course, Nicodemus, a member of the Sanhedrin, the highest judicatory in Israel. Educated, cultured man that he was, Nicodemus began the conversation both diplomatically, and at the same time, with a statement of the fact which had most impressed him. He said, "Rabbi, we know that thou art a teacher come from God, for no man can do these miracles that thou doest, except God be with him." In brief, Nicodemus was convinced that Jesus possessed a very special relationship with God, because of his supernatural powers, specifically his power to work miracles.

Jesus, however, interrupted the conversation, abruptly one might say, to declare, "Verily, verily, I say unto thee, except a man be born again, he cannot see the kingdom of God." Again Jesus said, "Except a man be born of water and of the Spirit, he cannot enter into the kingdom of God." Jesus was saying, in effect, that for a man to enter into the kingdom of God, or to put it another way, for a man to achieve eternal life, requires a miracle which is more profound and mysterious than any Nicodemus had yet seen. This miracle must be wrought in the very core of a man's being, producing a change so revolutionary in character that one might truly say a new man had been born within the shell of the man who had previously existed.

This revolutionary change, which must take place at the core of a man's being, that is, in his soul, we call regeneration, and the act of God whereby this revolutionary change is initiated, we call the "new birth."

Perhaps the most graphic portrayal of the new birth to be found in the Scriptures is contained, not in the New Testament but in the Old Testament. Ezekiel, in his prophetic book, records a vision in which the Lord took him by the hand and led him into a great desert valley. As Ezekiel stood at the mouth of the valley, he observed that the floor of the valley was strewn with dry and whited bones. These were the remains of the skeletons of dead men. After the prophet had had opportunity to survey the scene, the Lord asked of him, "Son of man, can these bones live?" Ezekiel, knowing the power of God, replied, "O Lord God, Thou knowest."

One is reminded of the words of Jesus that it is easier for a camel to pass through the eye of a needle than for a rich man to enter into the kingdom of God. When the disciples heard this, they asked, "Who, then, can be saved?" Jesus answered, "With men, this is impossible, but with God all things are possible."

Now we are to learn that God is able to give life to the

REGENERATION: A RESURRECTION FROM THE DEAD

dead, that he is able to bring forth the dead from their graves (cf. Matt. 19:24-26).

Thereupon the Lord commanded him, "Prophesy upon these bones, and say unto them, O ye dry bones, hear the Word of the Lord. Thus saith the Lord God. . . . Behold, I will cause breath to enter into you, and ye shall live." When the prophet had done as he was commanded, he reports that bone joined bone, that sinew and flesh came upon them, but we read, "There was no breath in them." Then the Lord commanded Ezekiel, ". . . son of man . . . say to the wind, Thus saith the Lord God: Come from the four winds, O breath, and breathe upon these slain that they may live." When the prophet had done as he was commanded, he reports that "breath came upon them, and they lived and stood upon their feet, an exceeding great army."

Consider the symbolism of the vision. The dry and whited bones on the floor of the valley depict the state of all mankind. This is man in the state of sin. Ezekiel saw but part of the picture to be certain, for he was granted a vision of the dry bones of the "house of Israel," that is, all those whom God would bring to salvation and life. Nonetheless, this is the condition of the whole of unregenerate mankind. Not only do we read of the race of men, "There is none righteous, no not one," but we learn the reason for this universal unrighteousness from the pen of Paul who declares that all died in Adam (cf. I Cor. 15:22). Thus, as we look upon the dry bones in the original "death valley," we know that we are looking upon the whole race of men who have become spiritually extinct.

We must learn that this is the root-cause of every problem which afflicts mankind, the corruption of spiritual death. The sickness of world civilization, every evil and ill which beset human society, and our personal and individual problems arise from this basic condition, the corruption of spiritual death.

In this connection, consider, ever so briefly, the account

of the prodigal son, the young man who took his portion of the family fortune and went out into the world to live a life of immorality and debauchery. Then, through a series of circumstances in the providence and grace of God, he was led to perceive the error of his ways and return to his father's house. How did Jesus describe what happened in the life of that young man? As Jesus told the parable, He put these words upon the lips of the father, ". . . my son was dead, and is alive again" (Luke 15:24).

It was not the wine, nor the women of low estate, nor the hog pen to which the young man descended that caused him to be a sinner in the sight of God. Jesus points out that something was terribly wrong within the young man himself. He was dead, spiritually dead, dead in trespasses and sin. It was the corruption of spiritual death in his own soul which sent him out into a life of sin. When he returned, the father knew that a miracle had taken place in his son. He had been dead; therefore, he had been content in the far country. Now he was alive; therefore, he had come home.

We must also understand, however, that the universal condition of spiritual death does not necessarily manifest itself in an immoral life or in low living. Several factors, education, culture, social restriction, these and other restraining factors, serve to camouflage man's true spiritual condition in the lives of many. The end result may be a man whose life is morally and ethically "good" from the human point of view, but whose internal spiritual condition is no different from that of the Prodigal.

This may be seen, if we compare the lives of such diverse men as the Prodigal on the one hand, and Nicodemus, teacher of Israel, on the other. The Prodigal was a dissolute young man. In our time we might have called him a juvenile delinquent, or perhaps, a young wastrel. Nicodemus, externally, stood at the opposite pole of human conduct. He was a man of education and breeding; he occupied an important position in the society of his day; respectability and prestige were his. Yet, these two were "brothers" spiritually. Just

REGENERATION: A RESURRECTION FROM THE DEAD

as the father was compelled to say of the Prodigal, "My son was dead," so Jesus was compelled to say to Nicodemus, "Ye must be born again."

We are so easily deceived by external appearances. How often respectability is mistaken for regeneration; social acceptability is mistaken for salvation; culture is mistaken for consecration; and prestige is mistaken for piety. Man "looketh upon the outward appearance," indeed, "but God looketh upon the heart." When Jesus looketh into the heart of Nicodemus, leader of Israel, he saw the same corruption of spiritual death which was in the heart of the Prodigal. I must say something to you now, and there is no kindly way of saying it. Whoever you are, if you are not living the new life in Christ, you are spiritually dead. Ye must be born again.

Next we come to a crucial point. Nicodemus asked, "How can these things be?" This ought to be the question of every seeking soul. If it be true that, except a man be born of water and the Spirit, he cannot enter into the kingdom of God, then we had best learn how these things can be. Jesus had in fact already answered Nicodemus' question, but Nicodemus had not understood yet. Jesus had said, "Marvel not that I said unto thee, Ye must be born again. The wind bloweth where it will, and thou hearest the sound thereof, but canst not tell whence it cometh and whither it goeth; so is everyone that is born of the Spirit."

No man knows the source or destination of the wind. We may temporarily determine its direction from the thrust of its force, but its source and destination are beyond our determination. More still, no man can control the action of wind, either to call upon it or to send it away. So, in sailing days, vessels were becalmed at sea. So, in our time, a tornado strikes a community, smashing down homes and buildings, leaving devastation in its wake, and man is powerless to stop it. So it is with the Spirit of God. Man is not able to call upon the Spirit to do his bidding; neither when the Spirit comes is man able to send him away.

If we return to Ezekiel's vision, we shall clearly perceive

why God must send the Spirit according to his own good pleasure and upon those whom He may choose. To this end we should note the similarity between the creation account in Genesis, and the account of Ezekiel. Of the creation of man we read, "The Lord God formed man of the dust of the ground, and breathed into his nostrils the breath of life, and he became a living soul" (Gen. 2:7). God created man; man obviously had nothing to do with his own creation; man was nought but an inert form, until God breathed into his nostrils the breath of life, and only thus did he become a living soul. So in Ezekiel's vision, the bones of the dead were drawn together, sinew and flesh came upon them, but there was no breath in them until God commanded, "Come from the four winds, O breath, and breathe upon these slain, that they may live." Then, and only then, did they rise and stand upon their feet, an exceeding great army.

In each instance it is God who gives life to the lifeless, and thus, we learn that regeneration is the work of God. Just as God created man in the beginning, and man was passive before the power of God, so God must re-create life in the unregenerate man, and the unregenerate man, being a spiritual corpse, is passive before the power of God. Only God is able to give life to the lifeless. Only God is able to bring forth the dead from their graves. This was the message which God gave to Ezekiel, "Thus saith the Lord God; Behold, O my people, I will open your graves and cause you to come up out of your graves. . . ."

This is the meaning of regeneration; this is the meaning of being born again; this is the meaning of being born of water and the Spirit; it is a resurrection from the dead. The spiritually dead are made to live again. This, clearly, is the work of God, not of man. No man chooses to be born from his mother's womb. This is something over which he has no control. Neither does any man choose to be reborn of water and the Spirit; this is something over which he has no control. This is the work of God.

If we keep the picture of Ezekiel's vision before us, of God raising the dead, we shall not go stray on the matter of regeneration. The words of Jesus to Nicodemus are equally clear; yet, they are often misinterpreted. Jesus' opening declaration to Nicodemus was, "Except a man be born again, he cannot see the kingdom of God." Later Jesus was to say, "Except a man be born of water and the Spirit, he cannot enter into the kingdom of God," but now He declares that "except a man be born again, he cannot *see* the kingdom of God." Some commentators equate these two statements with each other, as though Jesus were merely repeating Himself. This is not the case. In the latter instance Jesus declares that the unregenerate man cannot enter into the kingdom of God; in the earlier statement Jesus declares that the unregenerate man cannot as much as *see* the kingdom of God.

Why not? Because he is a spiritual corpse, lying on the desert floor of death valley. Recall the passage which speaks of men who have ears that hear not, eyes that see not, and hearts which do not understand. This is the reference of Jesus. The unregenerate man has eyes that see not; he is incapable of seeing spiritual things; the unregenerate man cannot see the kingdom of God; therefore, except a man be born again, he cannot as much as see the kingdom of God, much less enter into it.

Perhaps the most frequent misinterpretation of Jesus' conversation with Nicodemus comes at the point where Jesus said, "Marvel not that I said unto thee, Ye must be born again." How often have you heard someone expound the words of Jesus, "Ye must be born again," as though Jesus were issuing an admonition to Nicodemus to lift himself up by his own bootstraps. The common Arminian interpretation would make Jesus to say, in effect: Nicodemus, you must decide right now to be born again. This is preposterous. It was no more within the power of Nicodemus to be born again than it was within the power of the dry bones to rise up of themselves. When Jesus said to Nicodemus, "Ye must be born again," He was making a simple statement of fact, the fact that God must give life to the lifeless, the fact that God must bring forth the spiritual corpse from the grave by the power of the Spirit, if a man is to enter into the kingdom of God.

Do you know why so few people today understand that regeneration is completely and totally an act of God? I shall tell you why. They confuse regeneration with conversion. When a man is converted, he repents of his sin; again, when a man is converted, he expresses his faith in Christ as his Savior. Many people confuse these acts with regeneration, but repentance and faith are not synonymous with the new birth. They grow out of and follow from the new birth. One must be born again *before* he can repent of his sins and express faith in Christ as his Savior. A spiritual corpse does not repent of his sins; in truth, the unregenerate man does not as much as think of himself as a sinner. A spiritual corpse does not possess faith in Christ. God must bring the corpse forth from his grave. God must give life to the lifeless. And then, because life has been restored, man is able to repent of his sins and to express faith in Christ as his Savior.

Unquestionably you have heard many sermons, both from the pulpits of churches and by radio, in which the statement was made; "If you will repent of your sins, if you will place faith in Christ as your Savior, you will be born again." We must be clear that this is the precise opposite of the teaching of Scripture. To use a homely expression: it is to "put the cart before the horse." No man is born again, because he repents of his sins and confesses Christ as his Savior. Repentance for sin and confession of faith follow from the fact that he has already been born again. The natural man, a mere corpse in death valley, has, according to the Scriptures, a heart of "stone." He is utterly incapable of knowing his sins or repenting of them. He is equally incapable of faith in Christ. When, therefore, a man repents of his sins and confesses faith in Christ as his Savior, we know that he has already been born again. His repentance and his faith are products of the new life which God has created within him.

It is the new creature, who has been given a heart of "flesh," who is conscious of his sins, who repents of his sins and confesses faith in Chirst as his Savior.

Nonetheless, we have both the right and the duty to call upon men to confess their sins and to confess Christ as their Savior. This is the meaning of our commission, "Go ye out into all the world and preach the gospel unto every creature. . . ." At the same time we must understand that when a man responds to the gospel invitation, repenting of his sins and expressing faith in Christ as his Savior, that this is possible because, and only because, God in sovereign grace has created a new life in the man. It is the new man, the new creature, born of water and the Spirit, who is both able and willing to respond to the gospel invitation.

As we see Nicodemus stand before Jesus, we see the first stirrings of the new life in him, though he did not understand it yet. Nor did the new life emerge at this time. Later Nicodemus would become a convert. In the day of the Lord's death, he would come forward to aid in the burial of the body. Then we know that Nicodemus is indeed a new man, born of water and the Spirit. Were it not for the knowledge of this latter fact, we could not be certain that Nicodemus is a sincere, seeking soul as he stands before Christ; but we do know; we are given the information that Nicodemus was to become a true follower of Christ, and thus we know that he is a seeking soul as he stands before Jesus. In this seeking after peace with God on the part of Nicodemus, we see the first stirrings of the new life.

Consider Nicodemus' condition as he stands before Christ. In Nicodemus we see a troubled man standing before Christ. For all the honor which Nicodemus had won, for all the prestige of his position, a teacher of Israel, a leader of his people, there was deep dissatisfaction in his soul. He had come to Jesus to learn if this Man could give him the one thing he had not been able to obtain for himself, namely, peace with God. Consider, then, could the dry bones in death valley know dissatisfaction of heart and mind? Of course not! What, then, shall we say of Nicodemus? Why, that the Spirit of God was already at work in his heart. It was the Spirit, working in the heart of Nicodemus, which created the sense of inner dissatisfaction which brought him to Jesus. This was not the heart of stone, the heart which has no sense of sin, or sense of need for God. Here was a heart of flesh, beating within the breast of a troubled man. This can mean but one thing. God had already performed a work of grace in his life. The first stirrings of the new life were present. No, Nicodemus did not repent of his sin that day. No, Nicodemus did not express faith in Christ that day, but the dissatisfaction in his soul, his yearning for peace with God tell us that the Spirit of God was at work in his life. This is the only possible explanation. God had taken the first step in the redemption of Nicodemus. Whereas only darkness and death had reigned in his heart, God was now creating life. This is the work of God. To Him alone be the glory!

Even so I would have no one to be troubled because the Scriptures teach that regeneration is solely and totally the work of God. There is no need for anyone to be troubled, and I think that we can demonstrate this with reference to three categories of people. Consider, first, those who are believers, who are living the new life in Christ, and who, therefore, have within themselves the testimony that the Spirit of God has created a new life within them. You, obviously, need have neither fears nor concerns, not if you truly have this testimony in your heart. Along with a wonderful sense of the peace of God, you have an over-flowing sense of gratitude that God has done for you what you could never have done for yourself. He has created a new life within you. Once your condition was like that of the dead men in the valley of death. Once you were dead in trespasses and sin. Now you are alive, alive for evermore.

You must understand this truth. Unless you are vitally aware of what God has done for you, you will not give God all the glory in your salvation. I know there are people who

REGENERATION: A RESURRECTION FROM THE DEAD

like to talk about what they have done in order to be saved. As long as a man talks that way and thinks that way and feels that way, he will never give God the glory in his salvation. Only when a man realizes that God alone is responsible for his salvation, will he give to God all the glory.

Among the unsaved, we must distinguish between two groups. The first are those who are totally unconcerned. They have no sense of separation from God; they have no sense of need for God. They have no desire for the things of God. What more can one say? Not only are they dead in trespasses and sin, but they are content to remain so. In outward expression, they range from the man who is simply disinterested, and who will not become interested, to the man who is a militant atheist. They are content to be what they are; indeed, they will not be changed. Though we bring them the Word of God, though we speak with them concerning their souls; though we hold the dying and risen Christ before them, they are unmoved and untouched. They have no desire to be saved. They will not be saved. As Jesus Himself said, "Ye will not come unto me, that ye may have life." Their senseless hearts are darkened (cf. Rom. 1:21). Out of the depravity and corruption of their own hearts, they have willed not to believe upon the only begotten Son of God. There is nothing more to be said.

There is, however, another group or another kind of person among the unsaved. Perhaps you are among this latter kind. If you have a troubled heart, if you are seeking peace for your soul, you can rejoice at every word that I have written. You should realize that the Spirit of God is already at work in your heart. Your concern, the seeking of your soul may well mean that God has implanted the seed of the new life in your soul. You will note that I have not said with certainty that the seed of the new life has been implanted in the soil of your soul. This can only be determined as we watch for subsequent developments. If you repent of your sins, if you feel within you the compulsion to confess your faith in Christ as your Savior, if you enter upon the new life of faith and live it with increasing faith and devotion, then we can and will be certain that God has created a new life in you. If you are able to do these things, we will know that God has worked the miracle of the new life in your heart. For the present, however, we are unable to speak with certainty, but we do have reason to believe, from your concern, that conception may have already taken place. The new life has not yet emerged; you have not yet felt the driving compulsion to confess your sins on the one hand and your faith in Christ on the other, but there is a moving force in your heart which brings you to hear the Word of God.

In the name of the Triune God, Father, Son and Holy Ghost, I have been commissioned to offer you the hope that is in Christ Jesus, not presumptive hope, but real hope. I have quickly added, not presumptive hope, for if any man can go on his way week after week, month after month, year after year, without entering into the new life in Chirst openly and actively, there is scarcely any reason to believe that the seed of the new life has been implanted within him. Ah, but if there is real concern in your soul, if you are troubled of heart and mind and are seeking peace from God, then I may offer you this blessed word, "All that the Father giveth me shall come unto me, and Him that cometh unto me, I shall in no wise cast out." Come, then. Come now. As you make your way to the cross of Christ, the Father will come out into the way to meet you, and you will hear him say, "My son was dead, and is alive again."

5. Internal Calling: God Opens the Heart

For many are called, but few are chosen.
—Matthew 22:14
Moreover whom he did predestinate, them he also called: and whom he called, them he also justified: and whom he justified, them he also glorified.
—Romans 8:30
Now when they had gone throughout Phrygia and the region of Galatia, and were forbidden of the Holy Ghost to preach the word in Asia,
After they were come to Mysia, they assayed to go into Bithynia: but the Spirit suffered them not.
And they passing by Mysia came down to Troas.
And a vision appeared to Paul in the night; There stood a man of Macedonia, and prayed him, saying, Come over into Macedonia, and help us.
And after he had seen the vision, immediately we endeavoured to go into Macedonia, assuredly gathering that the Lord had called us for to preach the gospel unto them.
Therefore loosing from Troas, we came with a straight course to Samothracia, and the next day to Neapolis;
And from thence to Philippi, which is the chief city of that part of Macedonia, and a colony: and we were in that city abiding certain days.
And on the sabbath we went out of the city by a river side, where prayer was wont to be made; and we sat down, and spake unto the women which resorted thither.

And a certain woman named Lydia, a seller of purple, of the city of Thyatira, which worshipped God, heard us: whose heart the Lord opened, that she attended unto the things which were spoken of Paul.

And when she was baptized, and her household, she besought us, saying, if ye have judged me to be faithful to the Lord, come into my house, and abide there. And she constrained us.

—Acts 16:6-15

An understanding of the language of Scripture, both in its etymology and its usage, is often indispensable to a correct interpretation. Sometimes the original language does not easily lend itself to an English translation. Several different terms in the original, for example, are all rendered "sin" in the English; yet, each of the original terms has its own flavor. In such cases we do not capture the exact shade of meaning which is set forth in the original. In other instances a term or a phrase is used in two different ways. This would be true of the word "resurrection." In studying regeneration, we learned that the new birth represents a resurrection from the dead, a spiritual resurrection. It means that one who was dead in trespasses and sin has been raised to newness of life in Christ. Because many people are not aware of this fact, they are in a quandary when the Scriptures speak of a "first resurrection" (cf. Rev. 20:5-6) and thereby imply that a second bodily resurrection will follow. Because they do not understand that the first resurrection refers to the new birth, they erroneously assume that the Bible teaches two resurrections of the body.

In our present study we must also sharply distinguish between two uses of the same word. Perhaps we shall see this most clearly if we turn to two passages of Scripture in which the same word is used in two different senses. In Matthew 22:14 we read, "Many are called, but few are chosen." In Romans 8:30 we read, ". . . whom He did predestinate, them He also called; and whom He called, them He also justified; and whom He justified, them He also glorified." Unless one understands the use of the verb "call" in each case, he could erroneously assume that these two passages are contradictory.

In the first instance we are told that "many are called but few are chosen." In the second instance we are told that all who are chosen (predestinated) are also called, and further, they are justified and glorified. How is this possible? Does the one contradict the other? Not at all; there is no contradiction. The verb "call" is used in two different senses.

Let us spend a moment with each of these texts. When we read, "Many are called, but few are chosen," the "call" which is spoken of here is the "external call" which we have previously discussed. It is the preaching of the gospel, the presentation of the gospel invitation to sinners. As we well know, out of the total number to whom the gospel invitation is extended, only some respond in repentance and faith. These are the "chosen ones"; and thus we understand the text, "Many are called, but few are chosen."

In the Romans passage, however, we read, ". . . whom He did predestinate, them He also called; and whom He called, them He also justified; and whom He justified, them He also glorified." In this instance, everyone who is predestinated is also called, and everyone who is called is also justified, and everyone who is justified is also glorified. This, clearly, is a very different "call" than the first. To the first "call" only some respond, but all who receive the second call respond to it and are justified and glorified. What, then, is this second "call?" It is the "internal call" of the Spirit of God, when the Holy Spirit causes the human heart to respond to the preaching of the gospel.

All this will become more clear as we study the sixteenth chapter of Acts. Perhaps you have noted in our study of the "Order of Salvation" that we have drawn heavily upon the Acts of the Apostles and the Pauline Epistles. We have done so with a purpose. These two, the Acts and the Pauline Epistles, taken together, provide us with a history of the first century church in the time of the apostles. They afford us with an opportunity to witness the redemptive work of God as it takes place in the lives of real people in actual situations. Thus, when we discussed the doctrine of election, for example, we did not study it as an abstract principle; we studied

INTERNAL CALLING: GOD OPENS THE HEART

it, rather, as the elective purpose of God was displayed in the lives of actual people in an historical situation. We learned that as Paul preached to the people of Pisidian Antioch, such as "were ordained to eternal life believed." In the study of doctrine of "external calling," we also looked to a real situation in the city of Corinth, and we learned, though Paul was to preach the gospel to all who would hear in that city, God could tell Paul beforehand that Paul would see much fruit upon his labor, for God said, "I have much people in that city." So Paul was encouraged by the Lord, for he could know that he was dependent, not upon the will or the whim of men but upon the eternal purpose and good pleasure of God.

Now, too, we turn to an actual situation in the lives of real people to observe how God brings men to salvation through that spiritual experience which we have labeled "internal calling." In this study we must keep our eye fixed upon one person, Lydia by name, who is sometimes called "the seller of purple." We shall observe how God singled out this woman, touching her heart with his Word and Spirit, and thereby bringing her to salvation and life.

As we pick up the skein of the historical record in the book of Acts, the Jerusalem conference has just been concluded. Paul has obtained a new co-worker, namely Silas, who was to accompany Paul on his Second Missionary Journey. At some point along the way, perhaps at Troas, they were joined by Luke who provides us with the account in Acts. The first stop along the way was the city of Galatia where Paul revisited the Galatian Churches. Then Paul would have proceeded into Asia, but we read that "they were forbidden of the Holy Ghost to preach the Word in Asia." Next Paul sought to go to Bithynia, but again the Holy Ghost forbade them to go, or as the record puts it, ". . . the Spirit suffered them not." So they came to Troas, and there Paul received a vision in the night. In the vision, we read, "There stood a man of Macedonia, and prayed him, saying, Come over into

Macedonia and help us." And Luke relates, "We endeavored to go to Macedonia, assuredly gathering that the Lord had called us for to preach the gospel to them."

To clarify our understanding of the passage thus far, we ask the question: "What were Paul and Silas and Luke doing at this point?" One may answer that they were engaged in missionary work, or if one prefers other terminology, one may say that they were about to engage in the work of evangelism. They were earnestly seeking to present the gospel to the unsaved. In terms of our previous study, we might say that they were seeking to present the "call" of the gospel, the invitation of God, "calling" men to repentance and faith in Christ. This is the outgrowth of the Great Commission, "Go ye into all the world and preach the gospel unto every creature." (Mark 16:15). This Paul was attempting to do; he could not preach the gospel to every creature, but he could take his place and do his part in fulfilling the Great Commission.

Now we learn certain interesting and instructive facts. Paul would have gone into Asia, but he "was forbidden of the Holy Ghost. . . ." Paul would have gone into Bithynia, but "the Spirit suffered him not." This is on the negative side. Twice they were forbidden to preach the gospel in a particular place. On the positive side, Paul was presented a vision in which he was called to preach the gospel instead in a third place, namely, Macedonia.

We could ask the question, "Why was Paul forbidden to preach the Gospel in Asia and Bithynia?" but I think that we should find ourselves proceeding on a tangent if we propound this negative question. We must put the whole matter together. Then it becomes clear that Paul was forbidden to enter Asia and Bithynia, precisely because God wanted Paul in Macedonia at that time. This is beyond argumentation. Paul was not merely forbidden to enter certain areas; he was at the same time directed to go to the one place where God would have him to be at that particular time.

INTERNAL CALLING: GOD OPENS THE HEART

This poses a penetrating question: Since Jesus had instructed his disciples to go out in all the world and preach the gospel, why should it matter where Paul and his companions preached? Yet it did matter. Paul was forbidden to preach in two areas; meanwhile, he was specifically instructed to go to a third place, namely Macedonia. From this we can draw but one inescapable conclusion, that God has a very clear and specific plan of what He intends to accomplish through the preaching of the gospel. He does not always reveal to us specifically what is to be accomplished. Neither for that matter did He reveal his plan to Paul in detail; that is, God did not say to Paul; "You must not go to Asia or Bithynia, but you must go to Macedonia, because I have planned that a woman named Lydia will be converted there through your preaching." God did not reveal his plan to Paul in such minute detail. The Spirit merely forbade Paul to go elsewhere, and then directed him to go to Macedonia. Paul and his companions obeyed the Spirit on faith; then God, through the Holy Spirit, brought to pass his plan for the conversion of Lydia.

In short order we learn, step by step, just as Paul did, why God would have Paul to be in that particular place at that particular time. In Macedonia Paul went first to the city of Philippi. Paul found no synagogue in Philippi, but he soon learned that certain Jewish women had selected a spot where they met for worship on the banks of the river outside the city. On the Sabbath Day Paul and his companions made their way to the meeting place near the river. There they spoke with the women, presenting Christ crucified and resurrected as the Promised Messiah. As a result of Paul's preaching, one of the women in the group, and only one of the women in that group, believed. This was Lydia.

We cannot doubt but that this was the reason why Paul had been directed to Macedonia, and more specifically to the city of Philippi. It was the purpose of God to bring Lydia to salvation through the preaching of Paul. I say, we cannot doubt this. After all, Paul was specifically forbidden to enter Asia and Bithynia. Again, Paul was specifically directed to enter Macedonia. Here Paul preached the gospel. Here Paul won converts, and the first of them was Lydia. In the light of the specific manner in which Paul was directed to come to this place, we cannot doubt but that this was the purpose of God, that through Paul, Lydia would be brought to salvation.

This fact becomes increasingly clear as we study the record in closer detail. Paul preached to a group of women that day. We are not told how many were present, but it is clear that there were several women, perhaps even a sizeable number; the number, however, is unimportant to our purpose. We are concerned with one fact. All of the women who were present heard the gospel message from the lips of Paul. All of them heard the invitation which is presented in the gospel; yet only one of them believed.

How will you explain it? Perhaps someone is thinking, "This happens everyday. Whenever and wherever the gospel is preached, some repent of their sins and confess Christ as their Savior, while others do not. The experience of Paul with this group of women was not unusual. Anyone who preaches the gospel in our time encounters a similar situation; some believe; some do not." Very true, the situation is the same, but you see, the question has not been answered. We know it happens everyday, but now we are asking, "Why does it happen? When the gospel is preached, why is it that some belive but others do not?" The fact that it does happen just like this when we preach the gospel today makes the answer all the more important. Don't you see? If we can find the answer to why Lydia believed when the others did not, we will also have the answer to what happens when we preach the gospel.

Fortunately, the answer is spelled out for us in unmistakable language. This is what we read, "A certain woman named Lydia . . . heard us, whose heart the Lord opened, so that she attended unto the things which were spoken

by Paul. And . . . she was baptized, and her household. . . ."
Now do you know why Lydia believed? Because the Lord opened her heart!

Was Lydia a better woman that the others? Was she more spiritual than the other women? The answer to this question will bear great weight, for we must answer it, not only for Lydia but for every man who responds to the preaching of the gospel in our time. Two men come to the church one day. Both hear the gospel invitation. One responds to that invitation in repentance and faith; the other does not. What will you say of the man who does respond? Will you say that he was a better man than the other? Will you say that he was a more spiritual man than the other? In brief, will you seek to find the answer in man by making of his faith a work of merit, or will you find the answer in the working of God?

This is why we must answer the question concerning Lydia: Was some spiritual attribute present in her life which led her to repentance and faith? The record does not say that. In truth, we can be certain from the total teachings of Scripture that this was not the case. The Word of God declares to us, "There is none righteous, no not one: There is none that understandeth, There is none that seeketh after God; They have all turned aside, they are together become unprofitable; There is none that doeth good, no, not so much as one" (Rom. 3:10-12 ASV). Note carefully this description of man in the unregenerate state. One, there is none righteous, no not one. Two, there is none that seeketh after God. Three, they have all turned aside. Four, they are together become unprofitable. Five, there is none that doeth good, no, not so much as one.

Notice the universality of these statements; there is no room for exceptions. Lydia was not an exception; you are not an exception; I am not an exception. Lydia's internal spiritual condition was just like that of every other woman in the group; more, Lydia's internal spiritual condition was just like that of every other woman in the world, in her day and in ours. This is why it was necessary for God to open her heart. If God had not opened her heart, she would have departed with the others, unmoved and untouched by the preaching of the gospel. It was precisely because God opened her heart, and only because God opened her heart that she was brought to repentance and faith.

This fact becomes increasingly clear as we study the Scriptural teachings concerning the heart of the unregenerate man. Our attention is directed to the heart by the Scriptural declaration concerning Lydia's heart, that God opened it. What, then, do the Scriptures say concerning the heart of man? Many things. In Proverbs we read, ". . . out of it [heart] are the issues of life." (Prov. 4:23). Man is in the condition he is in, because of the condition of his heart. What is the condition of the heart? In Jeremiah we read, "The heart is deceitful above all things, and it is exceedingly corrupt . . ." (Jer. 17:9 ASV). A graphic description is also found in Ezekiel where God declares, ". . . I will take away the stony heart . . . , and I will give you a heart of flesh." (Ezek. 36:26). The heart of the unregenerate man is, therefore, a heart of stone, or to put it another way, the unregenerate man has a heart with stone-like qualities or attributes.

Because of this Biblical description, I call your attention to the stone-like qualities of the heart of the unregenerate man. The heart of the unregenerate man is hard, even as stone is hard. When I turned to the dictionary for a description of the word "hard," I discovered that the dictionary offers fifteen various definitions, but the first one was this, "not easily penetrated." How true! Isn't this an accurate representation of the heart of the unregenerate man? Unless God penetrates the heart of stone, it shall not be penetrated.

The heart of the unregenerate man is also cold. We commonly use the expression "stone cold." So the stony heart of the unregenerate man is, being a heart of stone, cold. By this we mean that the heart of the unregenerate man is cold toward God; he has neither love nor affection for God; on the contrary, he is at enmity with God. This is the declara-

INTERNAL CALLING: GOD OPENS THE HEART

tion of the Word of God, ". . . the carnal mind is enmity against God: for it is not subject to the law of God, neither indeed can be. So then they that are in the flesh cannot please God" (Rom. 8:7-8).

Again, the heart of the unregenerate man is dead, even as stone is dead. Stone is not only inanimate but inorganic; it is, in itself, incapable of change. Heat and pressure will produce a metamorphic change in rock or stone, but this is a change which is induced by external forces. This is the crux of the matter. The stony heart of the unregenerate man is changed only by an external force. This external force is plied upon the human heart by the Holy Spirit, the Spirit of God penetrating to its depths.

The Holy Spirit must penetrate the hardened heart of man. The Holy Spirit must warm and melt and move the cold heart of man. The Holy Spirit must bring life to the heart which was dead. This is what we are to understand concerning Lydia. The Spirit of God penetrated the hardened heart of Lydia, warming and melting and moving it in the fires of the Spirit. The Spirit of God warmed the cold heart of Lydia. The Spirit of God quickened, that is, brought life to the dead heart of Lydia. All this is comprehended in these words, "The Lord opened her heart."

This is what we mean by "internal calling." All of the women who were present in the group that day received the "external call" of the gospel. You may be certain that the preaching of Paul was directed toward all of them in the same way, just as we direct our preaching to all men in the same way. All of them heard the same message. All of them received the same invitation to be reconciled to God at the foot of the cross. All of them were called upon to repent of their sins; all of them were called upon to confess Christ as their Savior. Thus, they all received the "external call" of the gospel. One of them, however, received a second call from God. This was Lydia. The Spirit of God opened her heart. She alone received the "internal call" of the Spirit.

Now we are in a better position to discuss the two texts

with which we began, the one reading, "Many are called, but few are chosen"; the other reading, ". . . whom He did predestinate, them He also called; and whom He called, them He also justified; and whom He justified, them He also glorified." All of the women who were present that day received the "external call" which is referred to in the first of these texts, but only one of them, Lydia, was chosen; thus, she received a second call, the call of the Spirit, the "internal call" which comes to those who have been predestinated.

So will it ever be. Among those to whom the gospel is preached with its "call" to salvation and life, only some will respond. God does for them what He did for Lydia; He opens their hearts. He sends the Holy Spirit to penetrate their hardened hearts; He sends the Holy Spirit to warm and melt their cold hearts; He sends the Holy Spirit to activate and quicken the dead heart, and thus, the heart of stone is rendered a heart of flesh by the work of the Holy Spirit. Then, and only then, will it respond to the preaching of the gospel.

This explains why two other names have been used to describe the same spiritual fact which is denoted by "internal calling." The same spiritual fact is also known as "intrinsic calling." The dictionary defines "intrinsic" as belonging to the constitution, nature, or essence of a thing. Thus the "internal call" is an "intrinsic call"; it speaks to the very nature and essence of man; it is the work of the Spirit of God in his heart. It is also known as "effectual calling." "Effectual calling" speaks, not only to the nature of the "internal call" by indicating its effective power, but it also speaks to the end result of the "internal call," which is, that the man who receives this call, the call of the Holy Spirit to the heart, responds to it. It is a call which produces an effect, a call which produces a result in the life of the one who is called. When Lydia was called, she immediately responded. Why? Because the Holy Spirit quickened her heart, warming it, melting it, moving it, and thereby causing her to respond

INTERNAL CALLING: GOD OPENS THE HEART

to the preaching of the gospel as it came from the lips of Paul.

You see, "external calling" and "internal calling" might be compared to two highways which run parallel to each other for a time, and then the one stops; it comes to a dead end, but the other goes on alone. Both the "external call" and the "internal call" are mediated by the Word of God. Thus far the two remain side by side. When the Word of God is preached, however, the Holy Spirit activates the hearts of only some of those who hear. This is the point of division. The external call stops at the shell of the hardened heart of man, but the internal call proceeds on, penetrating to its hardened depths. Thus, the preaching of the gospel, the "external call," falls upon the ears of all men indiscriminately, but the "internal call," the Word and the Spirit working together, is given only to the hearts of some. Many are called by the gospel, to be certain, but few are chosen to receive the call of the Word and the Spirit in their hearts.

When we speak of the heart of the unregenerate man as a heart of stone which must be transformed into a heart of flesh, perhaps this causes someone to suggest; "This appears very similar to regeneration"; and therefore, he asks: "How does internal calling differ from regeneration?" The two are most intimately related to each other. In the new birth, a new heart is created within man. With the internal call, the Holy Spirit activates the new heart to respond to the preaching of the gospel. The response of man to the preaching of the gospel is the active expression of the new birth. When any man responds to the preaching of the gospel in repentance and faith, if it be true repentance, and if it be a true faith, we know that he has been born again, because his repentance and his faith are the products of the new life which God has created within him. So, you see, the internal call brings forth and activates that new life which God has created within.

Whoever you are, whenever you hear the preaching of the Word of God, the gospel invitation is extended to you.

Even now I call upon you, each and all without exception, to repent of your sins and to confess Christ as your Savior and Lord. If at the same time, right now, you feel a concern in your heart; if an inner voice declares to you that this is something you ought to do, indeed which you must do, then you should know that the Spirit is opening your heart. If this should be the case in your life, I urge you, even as the Word of God urges you, to do it now. Can you find it in your heart to repent of your sins? Can you find it in your heart to believe on the Lord Jesus and confess faith in Him with your lips? If you can do it, do it now, for ". . . if thou shalt confess with thy mouth the Lord Jesus, and shalt believe in thine heart that God hath raised Him from the dead, thou shalt be saved. For with the heart man believeth unto righteousness; and with the mouth confession is made unto salvation" (Rom. 10:9-10). You must sense the urgency of this matter. The eternal destiny of your soul is at stake; therefore, do it; do it now!

At the same time there is a blessed word of reassurance to those who have already come, confessing their sins and professing their faith in Christ as their Savior and Lord, for if you have been called out by the Spirit of God, then you can also know that God hath justified you, and He will also bring you to glory. You can know that!

At the same time I hasten to add that this is no word of reassurance to the careless or the indifferent. Why not? Because, if God has called you out, He has first of all created a new heart in you. You have become a "new creature," and this new creature loves God and worships God and serves God and is faithful to God—faithful unto the end. Hear, then, this decisive word, "He that endureth to the end shall be saved" (Matt. 10:22) and no one else. Now, therefore, if you have that kind of heart, if it is your joy and your life to serve God and your Redeemer, then I say that you can know, with all the assurance of the Word of God, that He has justified you, and He will lead you to glory.

If this be true in your life, and only if this be true in your life, then you have his promise that He will keep you unto that day when the General Assembly and Church of the First Born are gathered in blessedness forever around the throne of God.

6. Conversion: Repentance and Faith

And they said, Believe on the Lord Jesus Christ, and thou shalt be saved, and thy house.
—Acts 16:31

And the multitude rose up together against them; and the magistrates rent off their clothes, and commanded to beat them.

And when they had laid many stripes upon them, they cast them into prison, charging the jailor to keep them safely:

Who, having received such a charge, thrust them into the inner prison, and made their feet fast in the stocks.

And at midnight Paul and Silas prayed, and sang praises unto God: and the prisoners heard them.

And suddenly there was a great earthquake, so that the foundations of the prison were shaken: and immediately all the doors were opened, and every one's bands were loosed.

And the keeper of the prison awaking out of his sleep, and seeing the prison doors open, he drew out his sword, and would have killed himself, supposing that the prisoners had been fled.

But Paul cried with a loud voice, saying, Do thyself no harm: for we are all here.

Then he called for a light, and sprang in, and came trembling, and fell down before Paul and Silas,

And brought them out, and said, Sirs, what must I do to be saved?

And they said, Believe on the Lord Jesus Christ, and thou shalt be saved, and thy house.

And they spake unto him the word of the Lord, and to all that were in his house.

And he took them the same hour of the night, and washed their stripes; and was baptized, he and all his, straightway.

—Acts 16:22-33

Paul, an apostle of Jesus Christ by the will of God, according to the promise of life which is in Christ Jesus,

To Timothy, my dearly beloved son: Grace, mercy, and peace, from God the Father and Christ Jesus our Lord.

I thank God, whom I serve from my forefathers with pure conscience, that without ceasing I have remembrance of thee in my prayers night and day;

Greatly desiring to see thee, being mindful of thy tears, that I may be filled with joy;

When I call to remembrance the unfeigned faith that is in thee, which dwelt first in thy grandmother Lois, and thy mother Eunice; and I am persuaded that in thee also.

Wherefore I put thee in remembrance, that thou stir up the gift of God, which is in thee by the putting on of my hands.

—II Timothy 1:1-6

When we consider "conversion," we are treading familiar ground; the subject is frequently preached upon in evangelical churches; more, there is a large area of agreement among all evangelical churches as to the nature and meaning of that spiritual experience which we denote by the term "conversion." It is frequently described as a "turning," a turning away from sin and self and the world, and a turning to God. All Christendom further agrees that conversion consists of two constitutive elements, namely, repentance and faith. Thus, the converted man is one who has repented of his sins and placed faith in Christ as his Savior and Lord.

At the same time we must recognize that considerable confusion exists as to the manner in which conversion takes place. Some insist that conversion must be a dramatic experience, as for example, after the manner of an Apostle Paul on the Damascus Road. They insist that the experience must be so marked and decisive that one is able to point to the day and the hour when he first turned to Christ in repentance and faith. They will admit of no other possible manner in which conversion can take place, and therefore, they turn to us who have had the same kind of experience but in a different way, and they imply that we are not truly converted.

I have known adults, who had placed their faith in Christ and served Him devotedly from earliest childhood, who were led to question their salvation because of those who insist that one must pass through a spiritual upheaval in order to be saved. Even more disturbing is the experience of our children from time to time as they attend inter-denominational youth meetings. Occasionally the speaker will sneer at their relationship to Christ and the Church, because they are not able to pinpoint the day and date of their conversion.

Because such thinking is wide-spread, it is important for

us to understand, not only the nature of conversion but the manner in which it comes to pass in the lives of various people. To this end, we shall consider conversion in its simplest and most elemental terms, as it takes place in the lives of men under two decidedly different sets of circumstances. We shall consider, first, how conversion takes place in the life of the man who has little if any prior knowledge of the gospel. Then, both for the sake of comparison and contrast, we shall consider conversion as it takes place in the life of the person who was born and reared in a Christian home and within the communion of the Church. We shall make use of the Philippian Jailer, as an example of the man who comes into abrupt contact with the gospel in adult life, and who, therefore, did have a dramatic conversion experience. We shall also consider Timothy who was reared in the faith by his mother and grandmother, and who, therefore, should present a rather typical example of the man who was reared in The Faith as a child.

The case of the Philippian Jailer is too well known to warrant retelling, except in briefest outline. This was the man who was in charge of the dungeon in which Paul and Silas were imprisoned. He had placed Paul and Silas in the stocks and had gone about his business. In the night God sent an earthquake; the foundations of the prison were shaken, and the doors were wrenched open by the stresses created in the structure. The Jailer assumed that his prisoners would flee. If so, he would stand before the Roman tribunal, after the fashion of a court martial. Instead, he was preparing to take his own life when Paul called to him, "Do thyself no harm, for we are all here." It was then the Jailer cried, "What must I do to be saved?" and Paul made the now famous reply, "Believe on the Lord Jesus Christ, and thou shalt be saved, and thy house." The Jailer did believe, and he was baptized, "he and all his."

I think we may correctly refer to the Philippian Jailer as a "mission-type" convert. He apparently had no prior knowledge of the gospel. He was a life-long pagan; at the

CONVERSION: REPENTANCE AND FAITH

earliest, he may have heard of Paul's activities in connection with the incident for which Paul had been cast into prison. His experience was abrupt and dramatic, after the manner of the derelict who stumbles into the mission; and he would forever after be able to name the day and date of his conversion. If, therefore, we are able to investigate his spiritual experience, we shall learn some of the facts concerning other men who have similar conversion experiences.

What can we discover concerning this man? From the total body of Scripture we learn, first, that this man was ordained of God unto eternal life. In the thirteenth chapter of Acts (13:48) we learn that as many as are ordained unto eternal life believe. The Philippian Jailer believed; therefore, we can know that he was ordained unto eternal life. Lest there be any misunderstanding, let us have it clearly before us that this man believed, because he had been ordained unto eternal life. It is never the other way around; one is not ordained unto eternal life, because he believes; one believes, because he has first been ordained unto eternal life.

Second, he had heard the "external call" of the gospel. This undoubtedly occurred as he was placing Paul and Silas in the stocks. Knowing Paul as we do, we cannot doubt but that he was speaking to the man, even as he was being chained in the dungeon. How much time Paul was permitted in which to present the message, or to what extent he was able to present it, we do not know. One thing we do know, the Jailer had heard enough to realize that Paul could answer the question, "What must I do to be saved?" The very question indicates that Paul had talked with the man concerning his salvation.

Third, the Jailer had been "born again." Here, too, we must keep the order straight. The man was not born again, because he believed; he believed, because he was born again. If you were to ask me when he was "born again," I would reply that we can't be certain as to the exact time, it may have been when the earthquake struck, or again, it may have been earlier; God may have implanted the first seed of the new life even as Paul talked with him earlier in the day. If anyone should be thinking, "No, it could not have been earlier, because the Jailer did not repent or believe until after the earthquake," I would reply by pointing out that the new birth is to be distinguished from conversion, even though the two are closely related to each other.

In regeneration, God transforms the heart of stone and renders it a heart of flesh; this must precede conversion, for the man with a heart of stone will neither repent of his sins nor confess faith in Christ as his Savior. And sometimes a period intervenes, between the time when God implants the first seed of the new life, and the time when that new life responds to the invitation of God in repentance and faith. In any event, we know that God wrought a work of grace in the life of the Philippian Jailer, and as a result of the new life which God implanted, the man repented of his sins and confessed faith in Christ as his Savior.

Fourth, when the Jailer was reborn, he was at the same time joined to Christ in the spiritual bond which we call "mystical union." This relationship is so intimate that Jesus could say, "I am in you, and ye are in me." He could say further, "Without me, ye can do nothing." Therefore, when we see this man doing "something," when we hear him cry out, "What must I do to be saved?" we know that Christ is in him, and He is in Christ. Thus the bond was formed, and the Holy Spirit was at work in the heart and life of the Philippian Jailer, preparing him to respond and enabling him to respond to the gospel which Paul presented.

Fifth, we can also know that the Spirit worked in his heart in that marvelous way which we know as "internal calling." In the case of Lydia, whose conversion is described earlier in the same chapter, we read that the Lord opened her heart, so that she attended unto the things which were spoken by Paul. (16:14). The Jailer, like Lydia before him, paid heed to the things which were spoken by Paul; therefore,

CONVERSION: REPENTANCE AND FAITH

we can be certain that God opened his heart, and thus the Jailer came to repentance and faith. Out of his heart and from his lips came the great question, "What must I do to be saved?" And from Paul came the answer, "Believe on the Lord Jesus Christ, and thou shalt be saved, and thy house."

The pattern which we have just outlined seldom appears in such bold relief as we have set it forth. In the instance of the Philippian Jailer, and in the case of most "mission-type" converts, where an abrupt conversion experience takes place, the various steps may occur almost simultaneously. In truth, the whole pattern, including all the afore-mentioned steps, may appear to be merged into a single grand spiritual experience. All that meets the external eye is that the gospel has been preached, and the convert responded in repentance and faith.

This brings one to the decisive question: What is it that causes the conversion experience of a man such as this to be so sharp and dramatic? What element in the conversion experience creates the spiritual upheaval in the man's life? The answer should be clear; it is the suddenness with which the experience occurs. In the case of the Philippian Jailer, God sent an earthquake, and the earthquake created a crisis in the life of the man. In the instance of Paul on the Damascus Road, a light shown down from heaven and the Lord spoke to Paul, with the result that Paul fell to his knees and cried out, "Who art Thou, Lord?" I have seen a similar experience take place in the lives of a young father and mother when their infant child was suddenly taken in death. God transformed their lives in a moment of time. I have seen it, too, in the life of a man who lay critically injured on a hospital bed. God used that experience, crushing the body that the soul might live. Sometimes it takes place, too, without any external physical circumstance, when God opens the heart of an unbeliever, even as he hears the preaching of the gospel, and the experience in his own heart is so sudden and shocking that he is shaken by it.

Under these circumstances a man knows the day and the hour of his conversion. The experience is so swift and sudden and striking that he cannot be unaware of it. One moment he was an unbeliever, the next a man of faith; one moment in darkness, the next in light; one moment in death, the next in life. Note the suddenness, the sharpness with which the experience struck.

The experience is even more marked, if the man has previously led a dissolute life. The unconverted drunkard drinks no more. The converted thief steals no more; the converted liar lies no more. The man who has been a thief, an embezzler, or a business man without ethics will make restitution for his unscrupulous deeds. Such external changes are not only so revolutionary but so tangible that no one doubts but that the man has had a real, transforming spiritual experience.

Now let us consider the other type of conversion experience, such as came to pass in the life of Timothy. The record provides few details on the early life of Timothy, except for two notable facts. His mother and his grandmother preceded him in The Faith. The Faith was in their hearts, wrote Paul, and now I am convinced that it is in your heart also. Secondly, as a very young man, he was already an elder in the Church. Surely we do no injustice to the Scriptural record when we suggest that Timothy's experience was similar, in general, to that of many men who were reared in The Faith from childhood. In truth, the circumstances in his life are more typical, more common in our experience than the other. Why is this the case? Because most of the professing Christians to be found in most churches today are people who were born and reared in The Faith.

In the time of the apostles, when the gospel as we know it was being preached for the first time, and men who had lived either in Judaism or Paganism were converted, the more dramatic experience was the common one. The lives of men were changed and transformed in a moment of time, as men who had spent their lives in unbelief were brought to faith. This situation may be duplicated today in mission fields where the gospel is being preached for the first time. Occasionally it is duplicated in our midst in the life of someone who was not previously acquainted with the gospel, or again, in the life of someone who rebelled against The Faith in earlier life, but who returns to it through some dramatic experience in later life. Among us, however, it is not the common experience.

Consider, therefore, the experience of one who was born and baptized into the Church. We make no assumptions or presumptions concerning ourselves or our children. We have no thought that our children become the children of God by means of some mechanical or biological process. Paul writes that he had prayed for Timothy, and so do we pray for our children daily and every day. We pray the more diligently, because we know that only by a work of grace can they become the children of God. And we instruct them, teaching them about God, about their own sinful estate, about their need of redemption, about Christ who wrought redemption through his death and resurrection. We know that they must come to repentance for sin, and they must come to a true faith in Christ. In brief, we recognize that they must be converted; that is, they must pass through the same basic experience as the Philippian Jailer. We realize one more fact, however; because of the difference in the circumstances in their lives, the same experience will take place in a way that is quite different than that in the life of the Jailer.

Analyze the matter step by step. If ever they are to be saved, they must be ordained of God unto eternal life; if they are to be called, they must be predestinated. This we trust is the case, that is, we trust they have been ordained to eternal life, because of the promise which God has given to us and to our children (cf. Gen. 17:7; Acts 2:39; Gal. 3:7, 29). I say, this we trust because of the promise, but we make no presumptions, because we cannot know with certainty until later life when they demonstrate a true and saving faith in the living of a godly and Christlike life. It is to this end that we labor, and to this end that we pray.

Second, they must receive the "external call" which comes through the hearing of the gospel. This does not happen first of all at a public meeting or an evangelistic service; this does not happen, first of all, in a great municipal auditorium where a highly publicized evangelist is preaching; nor do they receive it first of all in the midst of a congregation of God's people as the Word is preached on the Lord's Day. Where do they first receive the call of the gospel? The answer is, this happens at their mother's knee, and as the father exercises his high office of spiritual leadership over the family. Among the first words they learn to speak may be the blessed name of Jesus. Perhaps the first little song they lisp will be, "Jesus loves me, this I know." They have heard it long before they come to a worship service, or before they come to a great meeting somewhere. They have heard it from their father and their mother, who have taken solemn vows, as their obligation under the promise of God, that they will instruct their children and see that they are instructed in The Faith that is in Christ Jesus.

Third, they must be born again. Our children are born in the same condition as all other children born into the world, with a corrupted nature which is transmitted from generation to generation, and except they be born again, they cannot enter into the kingdom of God. But when are they born again? Are they reborn in some great meeting, as they respond to an altar call, and walk the "saw-dust trail?" Generally not.

When you see little children who have already learned to pray in childhood, who even as children have learned to seek forgiveness and pardon from God, who have never doubted from their earliest memories that Christ is their Savior and Lord, and then as the years pass by, and they continue in that faith throughout their adult lives, when will you say they were born again?

Hear what the Word of God declares concerning Jeremiah, for the Scriptures declare that he was sanctified in his mother's womb (cf. Jer. 1:5). Not in a tent meeting, but in his mother's womb. He was cleansed of God. We must understand one fact concerning the new birth; it is totally the work of God. Man has no part in his own spiritual rebirth. Only God can take a corpse and create a new life in it. If this be true, and it is true, then God can create a new life in a seven day old child as surely as he can in a seventy year old grandfather. A new life, created within a spiritual corpse, is not the work of man; it is the work of God. The Spirit bloweth and listed where it will, and God creates a new life where He will. There are no barriers of age or of time; God creates the new life.

We cannot say in any individual case when God will create the new life, whether at birth, or earlier or later. This, too, is God's perogative. He chooses the time. But when we see the evidence in the life of the person, whether younger or older, we can know that God has done his work.

Fourth, the child must be joined to Christ in that marvelous bond of the Spirit called "mystical union." Either earlier or later, whenever regeneration takes place, even though we may not be aware of the spiritual fact at the time that it occurs, we realize that Christ must be able to say of the child or of the adult, "I am in you, and ye are in me"; and again, "Without me, ye can do nothing." When we see in the life of a little one that he knows already how to confess his sins to Christ, and when we see the faith and trust in his childlike heart, we can know that He is in the child, and the child is in Him, because He said, "Without me, ye can do nothing."

Fifth, God must open the heart. It makes no difference how old one is or how young. God must not only create a new heart within, but He must activate that new heart. He must cause it to respond, and this only God can do. When, therefore, we see one responding to the overtures of divine mercy, we know, no matter what the age, God has opened the heart.

Now we must note the total picture of the life of one who has been reared in a Christian home. As a little child he was under the instruction of the home and the church, as well as under the preaching of the Word. At no time did he depart from it or desire to depart from it. This does not mean that he has committed no sin; we all do, but it does mean that even as a child, when he sinned, he sought the forgiveness of God in prayer. At the same time, from his earliest youth, he has not doubted but that Christ was his Savior and Lord. This, his parents and his church taught him, and this he came to believe in himself and for himself.

As he grew toward adulthood, say for example, in the later teen years, he felt within himself the desire to enter into the communicant life of the church and to receive the sacrament of the Lord's Supper as a means of grace. He came before the consistory of the church. He had no vast overt sins to confess, but he realizes the bent toward evil within him; he has sought the forgiveness of God daily, and now he confesses before the men of the consistory that he realizes his need of the forgiveness and pardon of God. This is not a new insight, suddenly revealed to him. He has known this all through the years; he has asked the forgiveness of God daily in his private prayers for years, dating back into early childhood. More, he professes faith in Christ as his Savior. Nor is this a new work in his heart. He has never doubted that Christ is his Savior. He has known this and believed this all through the years, just as he has known his need of the Savior all through the years. He does not come to the consistory to make startling revelations. There is nothing shocking or dramatic about the situation. This is not something which was revealed to him yesterday. His father and mother had taught him these things years ago, and now he believes them for himself. There is no spiritual upheaval; why should there be?

He is not as a Saul of Tarsus who hated the church of Christ; there is no need for God to drive him to his knees in the dust of the Damascus Road. He has known his sin, and he has known his Savior from the beginning. He has not always served his Lord as he ought; none of us do; but he has always consciously sought to serve the Lord. Again, he is not as Peter who once served the Lord and later denied Him with cursing. He has never consciously denied the Lord; he has never consciously profaned or dishonored his Savior. To the contrary, from his youth he has sought to serve his Savior and Lord.

This man, too, is a converted man. Whereas he was born with a sinful nature which was "prone to hate God and his neighbor," God has created a new nature within him, if not at birth or before, then at some point along the way. This new nature has evinced itself through the years, as he daily sought the forgiveness of God when he sinned and daily gave thanks unto God for his Savior. He has no sharp and dramatic memories of a day when he fell upon his knees in the Damascus Road, nor of wandering into a mission door in a destitute condition. He only knows that his heart has been at peace with God from earliest childhood.

You see, the essence of conversion does not necessarily lie in a sharp spiritual upheaval; this usually takes place only in those who enter the faith later in life, and sometimes it is not a sharp and dramatic experience which they have. God has many ways of bringing men to himself. Some, God draws up short; these have the dramatic experiences. Others, God leads along more slowly. And some God has regenerated and led by the hand from earliest childhood.

This leads me to say a word to you who have been baptized into the church in infancy, particularly to those of you who have advanced to some degree of maturity. No one can prescribe an age level for you; it is difficult to say, in an individual case, when a person is old enough to know their own mind and heart; some children think they do; some adolescents think they do, when they don't. If you have been serving God for many years from childhood, if you have long ago learned to pray and confess your sins to Him; if you know in your heart that he is your Savior; if you no longer do these things, merely because your parents have taught you to do them, but if you do them because you have the desire to do them in your own heart, then you have every reason to believe that you are a child of God, and you must confess your faith before men.

Especially, do I ask some of you to consider your own situation. First, if you are mature enough to marry and rear a family, you are mature enough to confess your faith in Christ as your Savior. You who have come to this point, and who have delayed and procrastinated, must do some serious searching of your own hearts, if you have no compelling desire to confess your Lord. If you have one iota of honest concern for your soul, you should be on your knees, pleading with God for the grace to do what you ought to do.

If you are one of those who makes the excuse, and that is what it is, an excuse, that it is not necessary for you to come before the church and the world to make a public confession of your faith, you ought to be terribly concerned, and if you are not concerned, I fear for your soul. If you refuse to become identified with the body of Christ, you are, in effect, denying Him before the church and the world. Nothing you may say or think in private can alter this fact; He said of similar people, "He who does not confess me before men, I will not confess before my Father who is in heaven." You may attempt to delude yourself with the thought that you are his, but one day you may find yourself knocking at eternity's door, only to hear Him say, "I know you not."

If you are one of that increasing number who use the excuse of being "too nervous," I have something to say to you. I am aware that emotional problems can be terrible problems; I have seen enough real mental and emotional problems to know. I am not unsympathetic to your condition, but it occurs to me that one day you will be standing in the biggest crowd you have ever seen. Do you know where? Before the throne of God in the judgment. You will not be excused in that day, and you are not being excused now.

There is still another type; a few are usually to be found in the church. You should have come years ago, and you know you should have come years ago. In your heart you wish that you had come years ago; yet, you will not come now. You are too proud. This is the nature of your problem, your pride has formed a barrier between you and God. You are more concerned about what men may think than you are with the judgment of God. You will not be one day, you know. When you stand before Him who is the Judge of all the earth, you will forget your foolish pride; you will cry for the rocks and the mountains, but you will find there is no escape. With the Psalmist you will cry, "Whither shall I flee from thy presence?" and you will learn, too late, that neither in heaven nor on earth nor in hell can you escape Him.

One last word for you who say, "I am not ready yet," or "I am not living as a confessing Christian should." It amounts to the same thing. I have one question for you, "Will you be ready when God calls?" The Psalmist said, "So teach us to number our days that we may apply our hearts unto wisdom," and the first lesson we must learn is that we cannot number our days. I have conducted funeral services for mere infants, for a four year old child, for a teen-ager, for a young mother of twenty-six with three children, and for numerous others. God will not ask whether you are ready. When he calls, you will go. You get ready. You get ready right now. Not tomorrow but today. If the faintest breath of spiritual sensitivity is in your soul, fall on your knees and plead with God to take these foolish excuses out of your life.

Why do I urge this upon you? Because this is something you must do. Only God can ordain you unto eternal life. Only God can create a new heart within you. Only God can open your heart and cause you to come in repentance and faith. Ah, but then, you must do it. O, God is not helpless in dealing with you. If you will not answer the gentle voice of the Spirit, He may send a thunder clap into your life. He may drive you to your knees. He may wreck your life, in order to save it for you. Come then; come now; cease your kicking against the pricks, lest God find it necessary to drive you to your knees by some terrible and agonizing means.

If you can hear these words and remain unmoved and untouched, there is nothing more to be said, but if you have any concern for your soul, you should plead with God, plead with God as you've never pled before, that you may be given grace to overcome the barriers which Satan and your own sinful nature have erected, lest God find it necessary to crush your life in order to save it.

7. Faith: Given and Required by God

He that believeth on the Son hath everlasting life: and he that believeth not the Son shall not see life; but the wrath of God abideth on him.

—John 3:36

Now faith is the substance of things hoped for, the evidence of things not seen.

For by it the elders obtained a good report.

Through faith we understand that the worlds were framed by the word of God, so that things which are seen were not made of things which do appear.

By faith Abel offered unto God a more excellent sacrifice than Cain, by which he obtained witness that he was righteous, God testifying of his gifts: and by it he being dead yet speaketh.

By faith Enoch was translated that he should not see death; and was not found, because God had translated him: for before his translation he had this testimony, that he pleased God.

But without faith it is impossible to please him: for he that cometh to God must believe that he is, and that he is a rewarder of them that diligently seek him.

By faith Noah, being warned of God of things not seen as yet, moved with fear, prepared an ark to the saving of his house; by the which he condemned the world, and became heir of the righteousness which is by faith.

By faith Abraham, when he was called to go out into a place which he should after receive for an inheritance, obeyed; and he went out, not knowing whither he went.

By faith he sojourned in the land of promise, as in a strange country, dwelling in tabernacles with Isaac and Jacob, the heirs with him of the same promise:

For he looked for a city which hath foundations, whose builder and maker is God.

—Hebrews 11:1-10

One word spells the difference between victory and defeat, between life and death, between heaven and hell. That word, of course, is faith. The thing which divides men, the victorious from the defeated, the peaceful from the troubled, the redeemed from the condemned, is the attribute of faith.

The divisive character of faith is illustrated already in the early pages of Scripture in the lives of two brothers. Being brothers, they were reared in the same home and received the same training. When they grew to adulthood, they earned their livelihood in much the same manner, both of them living from the land, the one growing grain, the other raising sheep. One day these brothers appeared before God. Each had come to make an offering, a sacrifice for sin. Each, therefore, was aware of his sin in the sight of God. Each was aware of his soul's need for making peace with God. The one, Abel, chose to make his peace with God by offering a lamb upon the altar of sacrifice. The other, Cain, chose to make his peace with God by offering a sacrifice of the fruits of the field.

As far as the human eye could see, these two were as alike as "two peas in a pod." Each was aware of his sin; each made a sacrificial offering for his sin; yet, God accepted the sacrifice of Abel and rejected the sacrifice of Cain. Why did God accept the one and reject the other? Not, basically because, as some have naively suggested, the one offered a lamb for sacrifice while the other offered the fruits of the field, but rather, because the eye of God pierced the hearts of these men and saw what the human eye could not see; one was a man of faith; the other was not. One man accepted of God; one man rejected of God; the sole distinguishing characteristic: the attribute of faith.

We must exercise caution that we do not misinterpret the real difference that lay between these two brothers. To say that the one possessed faith while the other did not, is to speak about recognizable attributes in their lives. It does not, however, touch upon the purpose of God in the lives of these two brothers. We must understand clearly, therefore, that the faith of Abel was not a work of merit in his life; Abel's faith was the gift of a Sovereign God. To this end we must hear again the familiar words of Paul, "By grace are ye saved through faith, and that not of yourselves: it is the gift of God: Not of works, lest any man should boast" (Eph. 2:8-9). In this statement one has the fact in the case. Faith is not of ourselves; it is the gift of God; it is not of works. Therefore, Abel's faith, like the faith of every other man who believes, was the gift of God. Our first emphasis must be, not upon the faith of Abel, but upon the grace of God.

We dare not permit this fact to escape our attention. If we do, we shall find ourselves saying, "How great was the faith of Abel," when we ought to be saying, "How great was the grace of God in the life of Abel." Again, in thinking of two other brothers, Jacob and Esau, if we were to misinterpret the redemptive activity of God, we would find ourselves saying, "How great was the faith of Jacob," when we ought to be saying, "How great was the grace of God in the life of Jacob." This is the fact which Paul specifically calls to our attention in the case of Jacob and Esau, for he wrote concerning these two brothers, "the children being not yet born, neither having done anything good or evil, that the purpose of God according to election might stand, not of works, but of Him that calleth" (Rom. 9:11).

We must exercise care in another direction also. On the one hand, we must never forget that faith is the gift of God; it is the product of his grace. The Holy Spirit must create faith in the human heart, or we shall not have faith. On the other hand, we must not minimize the necessity nor the importance of faith. The Scriptures declare that "without faith, it is impossible to please [God]" (Heb. 11:6). Therefore, we dare not minimize the importance of faith.

FAITH: GIVEN AND REQUIRED BY GOD

God not only implants faith in the hearts of his people, but He likewise requires faith of them. This fact is set forth with clarity in the words of John, "He that believeth on the Son hath eternal life; but he that obeyeth not the Son shall not see life, but the wrath of God abideth on him" (John 3:36 ASV).

The concept of faith is, therefore, of the utmost importance in Scripture, and by the same token, the fact of faith is of utmost importance in the life of the believer. On the one hand, this seems to be understood by all of Christendom; few subjects are preached more frequently than faith. On the other hand, much misunderstanding seems to exist concerning the nature of faith. This we hope to clarify by pointing to the real nature of faith as this subject is set forth in the Word of God.

Probably the most tragic misconception of the faith concept is described by L. E. Maxwell in his book, *Crowded to Christ,* as "cheap and easy believe-ism." "Only believe," cries the preacher, but just what one is expected to believe remains vague and nebulous, since the same preacher scoffs at the idea of creeds or doctrinal statements. "Only believe," cries the preacher and dismisses godly living, as if Christ had not said, "Ye shall know the tree by the fruit," or again, as if the Scriptures did not declare, "faith without works is dead" (James 2:20). "Only believe," cries the preacher, meanwhile denying the immutable, changeless character and applicability of the law of God, so that for him and for his people there are no divine principles by which faith may be translated into life. This is the "cheap and easy believe-ism" of which Maxwell writes, a cheap-and-easy-believe-ism, one should note, which bears no relation to a true and saving faith.

Especially do I call your attention to the words of Jesus who declares that the "devils also believe and tremble," but neither their believing nor their trembling shall save them from the wrath of God. We do well, hence, to search the Scriptures for an understanding of the concept of faith as revealed by God. We are not concerned with what men say concerning faith; we are concerned with what God has revealed concerning faith.

The Old Testament is not as helpful as the New in gaining a comprehensive understanding of the faith concept. The Hebrew of the Old Testament contains no noun which can, of and by itself, be translated "faith." The original Hebrew of the Old Testament has a verb which can be translated "believe" and which is not far removed from faith. The Hebrew also has a word which may correctly be translated "trust" which is also akin to faith. Only in the Greek of the New Testament, however, does one find a term which embodies the full-orbed concept of the English word "faith." From an analysis of this New Testament term, both in its content and in its context, one may come to an understanding of the true meaning of "faith."

The first element in the concept of faith is knowing. This ought to be rather obvious; after all, one cannot possibly believe what he does not know. At this initial point already modern Christendom fails miserably. A generation or two ago it was deemed a mark of sophistication not to believe. The present generation has embarked on another course. Many profess to believe, but they do not know what they believe. Never before have there been so many confessing Christians in our country, and one may add, never before has there been such palpable ignorance of the Word of God.

When the question is asked: "What must one know?" the answers are several and variant, depending upon the theological bent of those from whom they come. Theological liberalism has no answer to this question. The theological liberal is certain that one must have faith, but when he is asked, "Faith in whom?" he has no ready reply. One of the best known ministers in America recently told a troubled soul, "Have faith in God and in yourself." How utterly impossible! These two are antithetical to each other. No man places faith in God, until he has lost faith in himself. Only when a man realizes that he cannot help himself will he turn to Christ in faith believing to receive the salvation of God.

When the evangelical is asked, "What must one know?" the common answer is that one must know that Jesus Christ lay down his life in atonement for the sins of men, rising again on the third day for our justification. This is Biblical; this is true, but one must understand that this answer is based upon certain essential presuppositions. One cannot know God as Redeemer, for example, unless he knows God as Creator. Neither can one comprehend the meaning of the cross of Christ, nor the necessity of that cross, until he understands the holiness and justice of God which demand the death penalty for sin. By the same token, one must know of the "fall of man' which evoked the sanction of divine justice. Again, one must know the love and mercy of God which parallel his justice and his wrath.

So one might proceed; indeed, so one must proceed, for the truth of God's revelation is one truth, and all the parts and aspects of it are intertwined and integrated into one unified whole. Ultimately one must realize that he must know the "whole counsel of God." This was Paul's declaration to the people to whom he had preached, "I have preached to you the whole counsel of God." Paul had so preached to them, because it is necessary to preach the whole counsel of God as it is revealed in the Scriptures.

When one is called to give testimony in a court of law, he is required to take an oath in which he swears to tell the "truth, the whole truth, and nothing but the truth." In this oath is expressed a principle, the principle that part of the truth is not the truth, the principle that a bit of truth mixed with a bit of error is not the truth. Even as the courts of our land demand the truth, the whole truth, and nothing but the truth, so let a man know the truth of God, the whole truth of God, and nothing but the truth of God.

One of the ever-present pitfalls in Biblical study consists in the temptation to take a portion of Scripture, a verse, a chapter, even a book, and to divorce it from the remainder of Biblical revelation. Each of the truths of Scripture and all of the truths of Scripture must be viewed in the light of the total revelation of God. This is the reason that our forefathers in the faith composed the creeds, the confessions, and the catechisms. Realizing the need for men to know the truth, the whole truth, and nothing but the truth of God, our fore-fathers in the faith drew together, bound-up, synthesized the great truths of the Word of God. They gave to us the creeds and catechisms as guides whereby we may study the Word of God and learn from it the truth of God in its wholeness and in its oneness.

I am aware that some hold the opinion that one ought to disregard the creeds and catechisms. You have heard their smug slogan, "No creed but Christ; no law but love." With grave piousity they tell us that they want only the Bible. Some even pride themselves on their ignorance.

Suppose, for the sake of comparison, that a young man matriculated in the law school of the University of Michigan. On the first day of the semester, the professor provides his students with a list of the texts they will be using. One young man raises his hand. "Professor," he declares, I will not need these texts. Just give me a copy of the constitution of the United States and a copy of the statutes of the state of Michigan; they are all I will need to practice law. The professor would reply, "My dear boy, you need to know the thinking of the great jurists of the past and the present; you need to know how the law has been interpreted in the courts of our country. It is not enough to know the law; one must know the interpretation which has been placed upon it." Perhaps you are thinking, "This is only reasonable." Of course it is; yet, the law student who would refuse to study the interpretations of the law is no more foolish than the Christian who refuses to consider the Biblical study of great men of God in ages past. These men, whose lives were bound up in faith and immersed in prayer, help us to understand the sublime truths of the Word of God in their wholeness and in their oneness. With their aid we come to know the truth, the whole truth, and nothing but the truth.

If the first element in faith is knowing, the second element in the faith concept is assent or conviction. It is not enough for a man to know. A man must have a conviction about what he knows, the kind of convictions by which men may live—and if need be, die.

As Paul stood before King Agrippa, preaching to him from the Word of God concerning his sinful life, Paul turned to him with these words, "Agrippa, do you believe the prophets?" Paul answered his own question saying, "I know that thou dost"; yet Paul left Agrippa that day an unsaved man, for though he knew the truth of God, and though in his mind, academically, he believed the truth, he had no conviction concerning it, and he remained an unchanged man.

Judas Iscariot provides a striking example of the worthlessness of mere knowledge if one possesses no conviction concerning it. No man had greater opportunity to know the truth about Jesus Christ than Judas. He was, above all, a witness to the deity of Christ. He had eaten of the food that a miracle had produced from the loaves and fishes. He had stood as Jesus' side as He healed the sick, the lame, the blind, and the halt. He was among those who sat at the feet of the Master as He preached the greatest sermons the world has ever heard. He had seen the winds and waves obey this God-Man, Jesus Christ. He had seen that the power of life and of death was in the hand of Jesus. Judas knew all that it was necessary for a man to know, but he lacked the conviction of what he knew, and great was the tragedy that befell his soul.

A problem is connected with the matter of conviction, the problem of determining whether one possesses the depth of conviction which denotes the difference between mere belief and a saving faith. This problem does not trouble the insincere or the ignorant; they assume that their "cheap-believe-ism" is sufficient, but sincere people are sometimes troubled. How shall a man know whether he has real conviction? Peter would not have become aware of his lack of conviction, had he not come to the courtyard of Pilate, and there, in a critical hour, denied his Lord. The Rich Young Ruler would not have perceived his own lack of conviction, had not Jesus insisted upon a true and saving faith which would cost him everything.

From time to time the convictions of professing Christians have been tried in the fires. The persecution of the Apostolic Church by Jews and Romans alike served to screen out those who lacked the conviction of the things they believed. The Spanish Inquisition, by its very brutality, purified Protestantism by culling out those who lacked conviction. The triumph of communism in China served to drive out of the church those who lacked the conviction of the things they professed. In the Latin American countries the persecution of Protestants works a constant cleansing in the Protestant Church.

How, then, can we be sure, who do not face these terrifying conditions? Well, first of all, the weakest, the least sincere, those with the least conviction, make themselves known soon enough. A few drops of rain, a few flakes of snow, a warm summer evening, and they prove that they have no conviction concerning the worship of God. Others are not far removed. They come to the church; they sing lustily; how pious they are—until the offering is received. Then we learn they have no conviction, no conviction which can loosen their tightly knotted purse strings.

For some the test comes in family life when a father, who may be seen in the church on the Lord's Day, does not take his proper place as the spiritual leader of his family. Or again in family life, when a husband or wife or both demonstrate a lack of conviction in failing to build a family life on Christian principles. Or in the world of business when a man demonstrates his lack of conviction by forsaking the principles in which he professes to believe for the sake of financial gain.

Someone may say, "These things are so small." I would

FAITH: GIVEN AND REQUIRED BY GOD

disagree with you. These things constitute the divinely ordained situations in which God provides us with opportunities to disclose the nature of our faith or our lack of true faith. "Still," someone may say, "these things seem small when compared with persecution and death. I am faithful in these every day situations, but if persecution should come, if hardship should come, if I were called upon to die for my faith, I am not certain that I would possess the conviction to stand." You are disregarding a divinely ordained principle: He who is faithful in small things will receive grace to be faithful in large things. And he who cannot be faithful in small things has already disqualified himself from fellowship with God. One must possess a conviction about the things he believes, a conviction that nought in all this world can shake.

The first element in faith, then, is knowing; the second element in faith is conviction; and the third element in faith is surrender. A saving faith compels one to surrender his life to Christ. This is the obvious import of the text, "He that believeth on the Son hath eternal life; but he that *obeyeth* not the Son shall not see life, but the wrath of God abideth on him" (ARV). Since this text teaches an important truth, perhaps we had best spend a moment with the original. The King James Version, which is so common in our homes, must be supplemented with another translation at this point, if we are to grasp the full significance of John's declaration. It reads, "He that believeth on the Son hath eternal life; but he that believeth not the Son shall not see life. . . ." Twice the verb "believe" is used in the English; yet, the verb is not the same in the original. The correct translation is, "He that *believeth* on the Son hath eternal life; but he that *obeyeth* not the Son shall not see life, but the wrath of God abideth on him." This is a significant difference.

From the correct translation of the words of Jesus, it is clear that the verbs "believe" and "obey" are virtually interchangeable. Faith, the only kind of believing worthy of the name, evinces itself in obedience. And obedience is impossible without faith. They are so closely inter-related that the one is impossible without the other. The man who professes to belong to Christ, who presumes to possess a saving faith, but whose life is not surrendered to the will of God, is merely deluding himself.

We shall see further the necessity of surrender, if we note its relationship to conviction. We have already noted that knowledge is the ground of conviction not only, but that knowledge must issue forth in conviction, or it is without value. Now we must learn that, as conviction is translated into life, conflicts must inevitably develop. When a man possesses conviction, his conviction will create conflicts, conflicts between the life he is living and the life he ought to be living, conflicts between what he is and what he ought to be, conflicts between what he may desire and the will of God for his life.

Unless these conflicts are resolved, they multiply, for as a man grows to know more and more of the will of God for his life, and as a man grows to see himself more as God sees him, that man will discover more and more points in his life which are in conflict with the will of God. This is inevitable, for the more a man learns about God and the will of God, the more he must be led to discover how far removed his life is from the high ideal of Christlikeness.

Sometimes, therefore, a man will appear to be Christian for a time; he will profess the Christian Faith; further, he may give evidence of a conviction concerning his faith, but one day his increasing knowledge of the will of God brings a great conflict into his life. There is something which he loves; suddenly he realizes that God would have him give up that very thing. He refuses to do so; he refuses to surrender; and his faith is broken on the rock of that conflict.

This is the story of Demas of whom Paul wrote, "Demas hath left me, having loved this present world." Did Demas believe? Of course he did! He believed with sufficient conviction to make himself a companion with Paul and to share

Paul's rugged life. Did Demas have real conviction? Of course he did, at least in some degree, for only a man of conviction would have shared the hardships of the missionary life as Paul lived it. What, then, happened to Demas? Simply this: As he journied with Paul, as he learned from Paul more and more of Christ, a conflict arose in his life. He found that his personal aims and ambitions, his personal desires and pleasures were more important to him than the things he professed to believe. At the point of this conflict, he refused to surrender; so the day came when Paul was compelled to write in sadness, "Demas hath left me, having loved this present world."

Now I must ask a question or two, nothing dramatic but exceedingly serious. You must answer for yourself in the secret recesses of your own soul. Have you ever, even once, said to yourself, "This is what I want to do, but this is what God would have me to do; therefore, I will deny myself in order to do the will of God?" Have you said that to yourself, even once? What was it the Lord said? "If any man would come after me, let him deny himself, take up his cross, and follow me" (Matt. 16:24). This is my question to you, "Do you deny yourself, for the sake of Christ? Have you ever, even once, denied yourself for the sake of Christ?

Have you ever said to yourself, "This is what I would prefer to do today, but God would have me to worship Him, and therefore, I will deny myself and worship God?" Have you ever said, "This is what I would enjoy doing with my leisure time, but God would have me do the work of the kingdom; therefore, I will deny myself and do the work of the kingdom?" Have you ever wanted something very much, a new home, a new automobile, a vacation trip, a night at the bowling alley, a day at the big football game, and have you said to yourself, "This is what I want, but the work of the kingdom will suffer, if I do what I want; therefore, I will deny myself, take up the cross, and follow Him?"

Perhaps this conflict has never arisen in your soul, because you lack the spiritual sensitivity to realize that such issues exist. If so, your case is, if anything, more serious still. Life is fraught with issues. Life is fraught with conflicts for every Christian soul, the conflict between what man is and what man does as opposed to the will of God. At the point of these conflicts, you must surrender to the will of God. This is faith, not only to surrender, but to be glad that you have surrendered as the peace of God floods your soul.

What shall we say then? Faith is knowledge; faith is conviction; faith is surrender. These three. Blessed is that man who adds to knowledge, conviction, and to conviction, surrender. To him belongs the kingdom of God.

8. Justification: Forgiveness and Imputation

> *For if, when we were enemies, we were reconciled to God by the death of his Son, much more, being reconciled, we shall be saved by his life.*
> —*Romans 5:10*
>
> *Therefore being justified by faith, we have peace with God through our Lord Jesus Christ:*
> *By whom also we have access by faith into this grace wherein we stand, and rejoice in hope of the glory of God.*
> *And not only so, but we glory in tribulations also: knowing that tribulation worketh patience;*
> *And patience, experience; and experience, hope:*
> *And hope maketh not ashamed; because the love of God is shed abroad in our hearts by the Holy Ghost which is given unto us.*
> *For when we were yet without strength, in due time Christ died for the ungodly.*
> *For scarcely for a righteous man will one die: yet peradventure for a good man some would even dare to die.*
> *But God commendeth his love toward us, in that, while we were yet sinners, Christ died for us.*
> *Much more then, being now justified by his blood, we shall be saved from wrath through him.*
> *For if, when we were enemies, we were reconciled to God by the death of his Son, much more, being reconciled, we shall be saved by his life.*
> —*Romans 5:1-10*

Two men went up into the temple to pray; the one a Pharisee, and the other a publican.

The Pharisee stood and prayed thus with himself, God, I thank thee, that I am not as other men are, extortioners, unjust, adulterers, or even as this publican.

I fast twice in the week, I give tithes of all that I possess.

And the publican, standing afar off, would not lift up so much as his eyes unto heaven, but smote upon his breast, saying, God be merciful to me a sinner.

I tell you, this man went down to his house justified rather than the other: for every one that exalteth himself shall be abased; and he that humbleth himself shall be exalted.

—*Luke 18:10-14*

Were it not for the principle which we are about to discuss, it is conceivable, humanly speaking, that none of us would be here today, or that this church would be here. This is the case, because we are about to consider the great principle of "justification." Surely I need not point out to you that this was the foremost principle of the Protestant Reformation: Justification by Grace through Faith.

A single sentence in the New Testament provided Martin Luther with the key to the recovery of the Apostolic Faith. It was simply this, "The just shall live by faith" (Rom. 1:17). From this great Scriptural declaration, Luther moved on in his thinking to another great New Testament statement, "Therefore being justified by faith, we have peace with God through our Lord Jesus Christ" (Rom. 5:1). And again, "For by grace are ye saved through faith, and that not of yourselves; it is the gift of God, not of works, lest any man should boast" (Eph. 2:8-9).

We shall not presently concern ourselves with Romanism, Protestantism, or the Reformation; we do want to consider, for its own sake, the essential and fundamental principle of "justification." This term and its derivatives: just, justice, justify, justification, lie at the heart of our faith.

This term, justification, takes one immediately to Calvary and to the cross of Christ. It leads us to a consideration of the death of the Son of God. Scripture uses many terms to describe what Christ accomplished at Calvary, and I think I shall not be contradicted when I say that the average congregation is better acquainted with almost any of the other terms than it is with this one: justification. We use the term "atonement"; by it we mean that the Son of God atoned for our sin, that is, He paid the price of our sin. We also use the term reconciliation; by it we mean that man, who had become alienated from God by his sin, was brought back into fellowship with God. And "ransom," whereby we understand that we were delivered from the bondage of sin. And "salvation," whereby we understand that we were rescued from danger, the danger imposed by the sanctions of God's violated law. And "redemption," whereby we understand that we were delivered, not only from sin but the penalty of sin.

But what do we understand by the term "justification"? Coming from the same root as the term "justice," you will sense immediately that we are about to consider the legal aspects of the death of Christ, or to put it another way, we are about to take a lawyer's view of Calvary.

Someone may object immediately, saying that what Christ did for a lost mankind at Calvary cannot be comprehended in legal terms. This is true enough in itself. One cannot fully explain the death of Christ in a legal deposition, any more than one can explain the love of God by a mathematical formula. At Calvary one comes face to face with the great issues of life and death and the eternal destiny of the human soul. One does not compress these things into a syllogism or an equation. At the same time, there is a legal aspect to the death of Christ, and no one will arrive at an intelligent understanding of the meaning of his death for our lives, until the legal aspect of his death is comprehended.

The legal aspect of the cross derives from the fact that man is a sinner, and he is a sinner because he has transgressed the law of God. From this initial fact, all of man's misery is compounded. Because man transgressed the law of God, he has defied the authority of God; therefore, man is a rebel upon the earth. Because man has transgressed the law of God, he has offended the holiness of God and is alienated from God; therefore, his need of reconciliation. Because man has placed himself in a state of sin by his transgression of the law, he is in bondage to sin; therefore, his need of a ransom. Because man is guilty before the law, he is under the penalty of the law; therefore, his need of redemption and deliverance.

JUSTIFICATION: FORGIVENESS AND IMPUTATION 121

All this Christ undid on the cross of Calvary where "He bore in his own body our sin." He satisfied the demands of divine justice by paying the full penalty of our sin by his death. Unfortunately, many people hold a restricted view of what Christ actually accomplished for the sinner. They think solely in terms of the forgiveness of sins. If, therefore, you should be startled by my next statement, I ask you to bear with me for a moment, for I must point out that this does not, alone and by itself, assure man of eternal life and blessing with God. You may ask, "If the price of my sin has been paid, if my sins have been pardoned, is not that all I need?" To which I must answer, "No, that is not all you need." If you were to ask further, "But what more do I need?" I must answer, "You need to be made righteous in the sight of God." It is not enough to receive the forgiveness of your sins from Christ; you must also receive the righteousness of Christ.

Permit me to attempt an explanation in terms of a financial transaction. Let us say that you have suffered financial reverses. You have not been able to meet your financial obligations; yet, the life of your family must go on, so you find yourself in debt to the grocer, the department store, the garage, and the utility companies. At this point a friend appears. He discovers your unfortunate situation and proceeds to pay all your debts. You are greatly relieved to be certain, but now let me ask you a question, "Does the fact that your debts have been paid mean that you have become a rich man?" You answer, "Of course not. I have nothing. It only means that I am out of debt."

Exactly! And that is your precise situation when your sins have been forgiven because of the death of Christ in your behalf. You are out of debt, but you have nothing! Yet, you must have "something," if you would enter the Kingdom of God. What must you have? Specifically, you must have a positive righteousness. Christ must provide you with something more than a pardon; He must provide you with his righteousness. His righteousness must be imputed to you.

Therefore, the death of Christ upon the cross involves a two-fold transaction. First, to put it in personal terms, my sin was put to his account. Because He bore in his own body my sin, the handwriting of my sin was affixed to the cross; therefore, my sin was put to his account. Secondly, and equally important, his righteousness was put to my account. In this two-fold transaction, He took my sin and gave me His righteousness.

This is justification. When Christ takes upon Himself your sin and provides you with his righteousness, you are justified in the sight of God. This should immediately raise the question before the mind of every seeking soul, "How may I obtain justification in the sight of God? How may I be justified before God?" Jesus Himself provides a concrete example, set forth in terms of a parable.

The parable concerned two men. Both of them were religious men; this we know, because both of them went to the temple to pray. When, however, we take note that both were religious men, we should not make unwarranted assumptions. To say that a man is "religious" is not necessarily to say that he is Christian; further, to say that a man is "religious" is not necessarily to say that he has found "peace with God." This is an important distinction which is too seldom made in our generation, the distinction between mere "religion" and The Faith which is set forth in the Word of God. We are too quick to accept the notion that any form of religiosity is acceptable in the sight of God. This, of course, is not true, as we shall soon discover in the instance of one of the two men of the parable.

The first of the two men is described as a Pharisee. As the Pharisee offered his prayer, we hear him say, "God, I thank thee that I am not as other men are, extortioners, unjust, adulterers, or even as this Publican. I fast twice in the week; I give tithes of all that I possess." This was his prayer, no more, no less.

In this man I see, first, the figure of the average unchurched American. He was thoroughly satisfied with himself. He makes special mention of the fact that he is not an extortioner, unjust, or an adulterer. This is the best method I know for soothing the conscience, formulating a list of notorious sins that one has not committed. From personal experience with the unchurched across the course of the years, I know that this is the practice which is employed by many unchurched people. Taking note of the fact that he has not committed any of the more notorious sins, theft, drunkenness, murder, and the like, the unbeliever assumes that he is quite "good enough." He is well satisfied with himself.

This man went a step farther however. He added the personal comparison test. He said, "I am not as this Publican is." Again I can testify that I have met and talked with a multitude of men just like this. Many is the man, and the woman too, who has said to me, "I do not go to church, it is true, but I am not like John Doe over there." The psychological principle is well known. If one makes the other man's character to appear black enough, he can make himself to appear white by comparison.

This man saw no need to seek forgiveness from God. Did you note that fact? Not one word of penitence is to be found in his prayer, not one word of sorrow for sin. Here one arrives at the crux of the matter concerning those who are outside the church, outside The Faith, and outside of Christ. There is just one basic reason why any man does not come to Christ and to his church. He feels, consciously or unconsciously, that he is quite good enough to meet God in the judgment just as he is. He feels no sense of sin. He feels no need of forgiveness and pardon. He considers himself to be good enough just as he is.

Secondly, I see in this man the figure of many who are within the church, that is, many who profess to be Christians. Does this seem strange to you, that this man could be representative of the unchurched and also of some within the church? This is true, because some within the church are not basically different than those who are outside. They may appear to be different to the undiscerning eye. Some wear a cloak of piousness. They have taken a thin veneer of religiosity and used it to cover an unconverted life and and an unregenerate heart.

So the Pharisee is like some within the Church. He added a little religiosity and piousity to his prayer. His full statement was, "God, I thank thee that I am not as other men." "God, I thank thee. . . ." His self-adulation was thinly veiled with religious overtones.

Then he pointed out certain religious exercises in which he engaged. He said, "I fast twice in the week, and I tithe my income." To some of you I want to say one thing at this point, "Don't sneer at this man, until you do at least as well as he did." When you are comparably faithful, when, for example you keep the Lord's Day holy, not for an hour but for all the day, when you tithe your income, then it will be time enough for you to look askance at this man.

Many people take an unfortunate view of the parable and of the Pharisee in the parable. In the corruption of their perverted minds, they reason like this, "The Pharisee fasted twice in the week; he tithed his income; yet, his heart was not right with God. Therefore, I shall not be faithful as the Pharisee was, and I shall not tithe my income, and all will be well with my soul." Such reasoning is born out of the utter corruption of the depraved human heart. This man was not wrong for what he did, but for what he failed to do. As Jesus said, on another occasion, "These [things] ought ye to have done, and not to have left the other undone" (Matt. 23:23). Therefore I say to you, have care lest you commit a sin as grave as that of the Pharisee.

For all the man's religion, there was something basically wrong in his heart. What was this? He had no conception of the fact that there is much to be forgiven in the lives of the best of men, not to mention the rest of us. Jesus said, "When ye have done all things, say yet, we are unprofitable servants."

If therefore you should be one of those select few in the earth who are, humanly speaking, unfailingly faithful to

JUSTIFICATION: FORGIVENESS AND IMPUTATION

God, if each Lord's Day finds you in the House of God, if you begin each day with prayer, if you live each day with justice and charity toward all men, if you thank God consistently with a tithe of your income—after you have done all this, if you have any sense of the supreme holiness of God and the utter unworthiness of man, you will fall to your knees at the close of the day and say, "Lord, I have been an unprofitable servant; be merciful to me."

Now note the second of the two men in the parable. He is described as a Publican, that is, a Jew who was employed in the tax-collection service of the Roman government. Hear the description of Christ, "And the Publican, standing afar off, would not lift up so much as his eyes unto heaven, but smote upon his breast, saying, God be merciful to me a sinner." Here was contrition; here was penitence; here was a sense of sin. Out of that sense of sin was born a prayer for mercy. And that prayer for mercy received answer from God, as the sincere prayer for mercy always does, for Jesus said, "I tell you, this man went down to his house justified rather than the other: for everyone that exalteth himself shall be abased: and he that humbleth himself shall be exalted." That man went down to his house justified!

Now, do you know how a man comes to find justification before God? He finds justification at the foot of the cross where he throws himself upon the mercy of Christ. This requires grace; indeed it does. The natural man is a man of pride. He rebels at the thought of pleading for pardon and forgiveness. He rebels at the very thought that his self-righteousness is but "filthy rags" in the sight of God. Only the Word and the Spirit of God can work repentance in his proud heart. Only the Word and the Spirit can work faith in his unbelieving heart, so that he will throw himself upon the mercy of Christ. And this is a supernatural work. Only the grace of God, using the instrumentality of the Word and the Spirit, can bring it to pass. In the light of this truth, we must see the Publican and hear him offer his prayer.

When we hear this man cry out, "God be merciful to me a sinner," we know that God has wrought a work of grace in his heart.

At this point we must note the order or sequence of events with care. The unobservant might suggest that God wrought a work of grace in the life of the Publican, *because* he had offered his prayer. The reverse is true. It was necessary for God to do a work of grace in his heart *in order that* he might pray this prayer. The natural man does not seek forgiveness for his sin. The pride of his perverse nature will not permit him to seek pardon. Therefore we know that the Publican's prayer is the result of the fact that God was already at work in his heart.

If one wished to press the point further, he might say to me, "But was not the Publican justified because of his faith?" Indeed he was. What you must perceive, however, is that it was necessary for God to do a work of grace in his heart so that he might repent and believe. Therefore, permit me to spell the matter out in the simplest terms. First, God wrought a work of grace in his heart by the Word and the Spirit. Second, the man repented and believed. Third, he was justified.

In the very hour that the Publican offered his prayer, two things came to pass. He found forgiveness with God, and he received the righteousness of Christ. Do not overlook one element in his prayer. You have noted his humility, his penitence, his plea for mercy, but this is not all. You must also perceive in his prayer the faith to believe that God can, and God will forgive. His penitence obtained for him the forgiveness of his sins. His faith obtained for him the righteousness of Christ. In the words of Scripture, "He believed, and it was accounted unto him for righteousness."

Note the correlation. We have said that two things are necessary to salvation, or to put it another way, that there are two elements in justification: The forgiveness of sins, and the imputation of the righteousness of Christ. And two elements are necessary in man, if he is to be justified. These two are repentance and faith. By repentance man obtains the forgiveness of sins; by faith he obtains the righteousness of Christ. Thus is a man justified before God.

This is not the end of the matter, for the justified man is one who is richly blessed of God. A number of blessings come into his life. I have called these blessings the "fruits of justification."

Paul writes, "Therefore, being justified by faith, we have peace with God through our Lord Jesus Christ." This is the first fruit of justification: Peace with God. How many people are looking for peace these days! No, most of them are not looking for peace with God, not consciously at least. They have not located the seat of the trouble. But who would deny that great numbers of people are troubled and disturbed. Though they are not seeking peace with God, they are seeking peace within their own hearts and lives. Perhaps a member of your family is in that condition. Perhaps you, for yourself, are seeking a peace you have not found. Let me tell you what the Word of God has to say about your condition. The Bible declares that the seat of your trouble is not, first of all, in the world around you, not in your job, not in your family, not in any external condition. The seat of your trouble is in your own heart which is estranged from God. When you have made peace with God, you will have peace in your soul and not before.

Hear me carefully. There is no little formula that I can give you. You will not find peace with God, nor can you find peace with God in religious mumbo-jumbo. You will find peace with God at the foot of the cross when in penitence of heart, you seek and find forgiveness for your sin, and by faith, receive the righteousness of Christ. In the day that you are justified before God, you will find peace, and not one day before.

The second fruit of justification is a new perspective on life. To be justified before God does not mean that all trials and heartaches will be removed from your life, but it does mean that you will view your problems in a different manner than you ever have before. You will learn for the first time that your trials are designed of God, not to hurt you but to help you, not to cast you down but to lift you up, not to curse you but to bless you. Paul put it this way, "we glory in tribulations also; knowing that tribulation worketh patience; And patience [worketh] experience; and experience [worketh] hope; And hope maketh not ashamed; because the love of God is shed abroad in our hearts..." (Rom. 5:3-5).

We glory in tribulation; that is, we not only accept our trials but are grateful for them, because we know the spiritual values which grow out of the very elements in life which seem hard and difficult. From our trials we learn patience, because it is the experience of the Christian that, if he will wait upon the Lord in faith, not attempting to hasten the unfolding of the plan of God for his life, God will lift his burdens in due time.

"Patience [worketh] experience"; that is, the experience of God's providential care over the lives of his children. As the Christian passes from one experience to another, he becomes increasingly aware that the hand of God is upon his life. He learns from experience that, even in the seemingly untoward circumstances of life, God is directing the course of his life to a good end.

"Experience [worketh] hope"; this is true, because as we pass from one trying situation to another, we have learned that God brings each one to a good end; therefore, as new and difficult situations develop in our lives, we can pass through our darkest days, being certain that God will also bring each new and difficult experience to a good end.

"And hope maketh not ashamed." The unbeliever turns to us with the comment, "Your life is not different than mine. We have both our trials and troubles. What, then, is the advantage in being a Christian?" Ah, but we know what he does not. We have had experience with God. We know from experience that God never forsakes his own. Therefore, while the unbeliever frets and complains, we move with confidence through our darkest hours. We are not ashamed of our faith or of our hope; we know that our lives are in the hand of God, and He will do for us only good and never evil.

"For the love of God is shed abroad in our hearts." We have this assurance, because the certainty of God's love for us is in our hearts. By faith we have assurance of divine favor, so that even when the condition of our lives is such that the world of unbelief would say we are cursed rather than blessed, we know better; we know that all these things are the working of the love of God, even when we do not understand or comprehend. Briefly and simply, we have the assurance that God is "for us." And "If God be for us, who can be against us? . . . It is God that justifieth. . . . Who shall lay anything to the charge of God's elect?" (Rom. 8:31-34). If God be for us, who can be against us!

Finally, "we rejoice in the hope of the glory of God." This is the crowning aspect of the Christian Life. The unbeliever may say to me, "Christian, wherein is your life different from mine? Our bodies are afflicted by the same diseases. Our lives are troubled by the same circumstances. And no matter what the course of our lives, at the end is the grave." I answer, "True, all true, but there is one vast difference; I have the hope of glory. I have a promise from my Lord, 'he that believeth on me, though he were dead, yet shall he live, and he that liveth and believeth on me shall never die.' "

> All the way my Savior leads me;
> What have I to ask beside?
> Can I doubt his tender mercy,
> Who through life has been my guide?
> Heavenly peace, divinest comfort,
> Here by faith in Him to dwell,
> For I know, whate'er befall me,
> Jesus doeth all things well.
>
> All the way my Savior leads me;
> Oh, the fullness of His love,

Perfect rest to me is promised
In my Father's house above.
When my spirit, clothed immortal,
Wings its flight to realms of day,
This my song through endless ages;
Jesus led me all the way.

9. Sanctification: Mortification and Nurture

> *When I was a child, I spake as a child, I understood as a child, I thought as a child: but when I became a man, I put away childish things.*
> —*I Corinthians 13:11*
>
> *If ye then be risen with Christ, seek those things which are above, where Christ sitteth on the right hand of God.*
> *Set your affection on things above, not on things on the earth.*
> *For ye are dead, and your life is hid with Christ in God.*
> *When Christ, who is our life, shall appear, then shall ye also appear with him in glory.*
> *Mortify therefore your members which are upon the earth; fornication, uncleanness, inordinate affection, evil concupiscence, and covetousness, which is idolatry:*
> *For which things' sake the wrath of God cometh on the children of disobedience:*
> *In the which ye also walked sometime, when ye lived in them.*
> *But now ye also put off all these; anger, wrath, malice, blasphemy, filthy communication out of your mouth.*
> *Lie not one to another, seeing that ye have put off the old man with his deeds;*
> *And have put on the new man, which is renewed in knowledge after the image of him that created him:*

Where there is neither Greek nor Jew, circumcision nor uncircumcision, Barbarian, Scythian, bond nor free; but Christ is all, and in all.

Put on therefore, as the elect of God, holy and beloved, bowels of mercies, kindness, humbleness of mind, meekness, long-suffering;

Forbearing one another, and forgiving one another, if any man have a quarrel against any: even as Christ forgave you, so also do ye.

And above all these things put on charity, which is the bond of perfectness.

And let the peace of God rule in your hearts, to the which also ye are called in one body; and be ye thankful.

Let the word of Christ dwell in you richly in all wisdom; teaching and admonishing one another in psalms and hymns and spiritual songs, singing with grace in your hearts to the Lord.

And whatsoever ye do in word or deed, do all in the name of the Lord Jesus, giving thanks to God and the Father by him.

—*Colossians 3:1-17*

In the days immediately preceding one of the more recent elections, a letter appeared in the "Letters to the Editor" section of one of the daily papers. The letter read, "I shall be voting for Mr. So-and-so for governor (or senator or whatever office it may have been). I am seventy-eight years of age, and I ought to know how to select a candidate." Perhaps my amusement at reading the letter causes me to recall it even now. "I am seventy-eight years of age, and I ought to know how to select a candidate." Herein was enunciated the age old doctrine that age, mere chronological age, enhances a man's capabilities and capacities. The implication was that this man was more capable of selecting a candidate, because he was seventy-eight years of age than another man who is, say, fifty-eight years of age, or than still another man who is, say, thirty-eight years of age.

This concept may be found in the Constitution of the United States, for the Constitution contains a provision that no man shall be a candidate for the presidency of the United States, until he has attained the age of thirty-five years. This provision surely implies that, in the opinion of the framers of the Constitution of the United States, a man of less than thirty-five years would not be capable of executing the high office of the presidency.

No one would question, I think the assertion that age, and the experience that is gained with age, ought to carry with them certain advantages and advancements. We must move with caution, however, before we come to any hard-and-fast conclusions about the matter.

History tells the story of at least some young men who reached the peak of their potential at a very early age. Alexander the Great is said to have conquered all the world that he knew at the age of thirty-two years, and then, according to legend at least, he is reputed to have wept for more worlds to conquer. John Calvin wrote what is probably the greatest theological treatise ever to come from the pen of man at the age of twenty-six years; this was his "Institutes." Calvin was a prolific writer; he produced vast quantities of theological material in his more advanced years, and yet, I think that any student of theology would agree that none of these surpassed his "Institutes," written at the age of twenty-six years. The supreme example, of course, was Jesus Christ. We hesitate to compare Him with mere men, even though He was Man as well as God; yet, we know that, at something under thirty-three years of age, He struck the blow that has been heard 'round the world for twenty centuries; more, its reverberations will continue through-out eternity.

We are all aware of these facts; so were our forefathers in the faith; yet, it is only in more recent years that psychologists have discovered the reason behind the fact that chronological age in itself may be quite meaningless. Psychologists have learned that all aspects of the human personality do not develop simultaneously; that is, a man may be an adult physically, but he may still be a child mentally; or again, a man may be an adult both physically and mentally, but he may be a child emotionally.

Today, psychologists, doctors, and educators speak of several kinds of age; physical or physiological age, mental age, emotional age, social-adjustment age, and the like. The rate of maturation in each of these areas may be different from the others. Thus a man may be twenty years of age by the calendar, eighteen years of age physiologically, fifteen years of age mentally, thirteen years of age emotionally, and his social adjustment might be that of a ten year old child.

We would not be discussing these secular matters, as important as they may be, were it not for the fact that they shed light upon an important Biblical consideration. There is also a factor in man which may be denominated "spiritual age." Paul referred to this fact as follows, "When I was a child, I spoke as a child, I thought as a child, I felt as a child; but now that I have become a man, I have put away childish things." It should be clear that Paul was not discussing mere chronological age, nor even mental or emotional age. He most assuredly was not speaking of putting away his childhood toys. Paul was referring to the fact that he had once been a child in the faith, or to use another of Paul's expressions, "a babe in Christ." Thus Paul spoke of feeding the "babes" in the faith with the "milk" of the Word. Now Paul tells us that he has grown up, or to use his own expression, that he has become a "man." He has passed through spiritual infancy, spiritual childhood, spiritual adolescence, and he has now become a mature adult in the faith.

Paul declares, further, that because this is the case, he no longer thinks or feels or speaks as he once did. When he was a spiritual child, he had certain thoughts and feelings and forms of speech. Now that he has become a spiritual adult, he has put behind him these marks of his spiritual childhood. He thinks, he feels, and he speaks as one who is a mature, adult Christian.

This process of spiritual development is called "sanctification." Sanctification, as the term is commonly used, may be defined as spiritual growth, growing away from what we were before we came under the power and influence of Christ, and at the same time, growing more and more into the stature of Christ.

One fact we must grasp, however, before we consider the matter of sanctification in more detail. Sanctification is not the beginning of the Christian life. The Christian life begins in our conscious experience with conversion. The unconverted man cannot engage in the process of sanctification, precisely because he has not been converted. Until a man has been brought to a conviction of sin, so that he repents of his sin, and places faith in Christ as his Savior, he will have neither concern nor desire for spiritual growth.

Apparently this fact has escaped the attention of many. In groups which we rather loosely designate as "liberal" or "modern," the issue of conversion is not raised as men are invited into the church. Sin and repentance for sin are never mentioned. A similar silence prevails with reference to the necessity of deliverance from sin through the shed blood of Christ. Instead, they speak of "character building." The seriousness of their error lies in the presumption that it is possible to build Christian character in the life of the unconverted man.

Where does this fallacy begin? It begins with the notion that man is basically "good." He may have some evil in him; he may do what is wrong, but underneath the error of his ways lies an essential goodness. Because they believe the nature of man is good rather than evil, they see no need for man to be transformed through the regenerating power of the new birth. The evil which man does is regarded as a mere error induced by his environment or by improper training. Since, then, man is good, his only need is to be educated. The purpose of the educational process is to bring out the good that is inherent in man from birth. Thus, the theological liberal may speak of man's need for growth or improvement, but he means something very different than do we who espouse the Biblical faith.

We know that man is not an intermixture of good and evil. The Word of God declares of man that he is "brought forth in iniquity and conceived in sin" (cf. Ps. 51:5); "There is none righteous, no, not one: . . . there is none that seeketh after God . . . there is none that doeth good, no, not [so much as] one" (Rom. 3:10-12). Further, man is not merely the victim of circumstance, environment, or training. He has within him a nature which is perverse and corrupt, because he is spiritually dead (cf. Eph. 2:1). Thus we know that a man must be transformed by the regenerating power of the Holy Spirit. It is the new nature, the new man who repents of sin and knows faith in Christ as his Savior. And it is this new man, and only this new man, who is capable of true godliness. Only this new man is capable of growing into the stature of Christ. From the Biblical point of view, this is beyond question. The seed must be planted before it can grow. The new life must exist before it can be nurtured. Further, we must make no mistake about the matter of character. Character is important. The greater the degree of sanctification of the individual, the higher will be the ethical and moral level of his life. At the same time, character, in the sense of morality and ethics, can be misleading, because it is external. Character can be nothing more than a veneer which covers a deplorable spiritual condition within the man. In this sense, education, culture, and the socializing of the individual can be most deceptive. A man can be taught to display habits and attitudes which belie his true spiritual condition. This is especially true in a country such as our own which has a culture containing many Christian elements. A man can act sufficiently like a Christian to deceive other men, though his heart remains corrupt. Of course, he cannot deceive God "who looketh upon the heart." And in the light of eternity, this is the only important consideration—not what men think, but the judgment of God. And God judges the inner man as well as the outer man. The inner man must undergo a spiritual transformation, if he is to become acceptable in the sight of God. This spiritual transformation issues forth in repentance and faith; thus, the man becomes a convert. Then, and only then, can he develop truly Christian character, which is to grow into the stature of the likeness of Christ.

There is a second essential consideration. Only as we are joined to Christ will we receive the power whereby to grow into the stature of Christ. You see, there are two elements in sanctification, both of which require divine power for their accomplishment. They are closely related to each other, and yet, we must distinguish between them. The first is commonly called the "mortification" of the "old man." By this we mean that we must constantly restrain and put down the "old man" who remains within for as long as we live in this world. Only in death are we completely freed from the old sinful nature. It is this "old man," this old sinful nature, which constantly seeks to impel us to do that which is evil. It is this "old man" within us who seeks to withhold us from doing the will of God. Thus, our "old man" must be mortified, that is, put to death insofar as that is possible in our lives by the grace of God.

This, as any Christian will testify, is no simple task. Paul spoke of this fact when he wrote of himself, "That which I would not, I do; and that which I would, I do not" (Rom. 7:19). The new Paul, the converted man, desired to sin not; yet, he often did. The new Paul, the converted man, desired to do the will of God; yet, he often failed to do it, because the old sinful nature remained within him still.

The "old man" makes a constant battleground of our lives. What a struggle it is to put him down. In truth, it is a humanly impossible struggle; only Christ can give us strength to gain the victory over the old sinful nature within us. How often have you heard the text, "I can do all things through Christ which strengtheneth me"? (Phil. 4:13). Why, then, do we so seldom hear his word, "Without me, ye can do nothing"? (John 15:5). This is the lesson of the vine and the branches. He is the vine; we are the branches. Only as the life and strength of the vine flows into the branch, is the branch enabled to bear fruit. Thus, we are dependent upon Christ, not only for the new life in itself, but for the growth of the new life within us. And only as the new life grows, is the old life put down.

This leads us to the second consideration. Even as we mortify the old man within us, we are to nurture the new life, the new man, who has been created within us by the Word and Spirit of God. Once the new life has been initiated within us, it must grow. Hear me with care; I did not say, "It should grow"; I did not say, "It ought to grow"; I said, "It must grow."

I place emphasis upon this fact for two reasons. First, some mistaken people are victimized by the notion that once they have made public acknowledgement of their faith, once they have become members of the church, they have arrived; they have achieved; nothing more needs to be done;

all is well with their souls. Permit me to point out with great emphasis, therefore, that this is but the beginning, not the end of the Christian life. Once you have had a conversion experience, you have only begun to walk the road of the Christian life, and you must walk not only onward but upward for as long as God permits you to remain in the world.

The second reason for emphasizing this fact is a misunderstanding on the part of some concerning the task of the church. You have heard people say, "We ought to be more evangelistic." Sincere and devout people have said, "We ought to extend a gospel invitation at every service." To this, let me make two replies. First, we want to so conduct every service that no man can come into our church without being brought face to face with Jesus Christ. Secondly, however, we must realize that leading a man to Christ is but the first step; after that, we have a duty toward Christ and toward that man, to teach him all that Christ requires of him as a disciple. This is the second great task of the church, the edification of the saints to the end that they may be increasingly sanctified.

I feel constrained to point to another fact of which many of our people seem unaware. In groups which place all the emphasis upon evangelism, and little or no emphasis upon spiritual growth, the people often have deplorable standards of ethics and morality. This is not a snide remark; it is an observable fact. It is these people who often bring grave dishonor upon the church, and in so doing, they bring grave dishonor upon Christ. They are quick to bear witness with their lips, but their day-to-day lives often tell a very different story. Sometimes I wonder, if they do not drive as many people away from Christ and the Church by their failure to display truly Christian character, as they bring to Christ and the Church with their appeals.

For each of us conversion is but a point of beginning. You may be a youth or in the middle years or an elderly person who has recently come into the faith. Your calendar years are irrelevant in terms of the spiritual life. Whether one is seventeen years of age or seventy, he may be but a babe in Christ.

From this initial point growth must begin. It does not take place mechanically or automatically. Growth in the Christian faith is consciously achieved by those who work at the matter of spiritual development. To consider a hypothetical case, let us say that two young men once desired to make public profession of their relationship to Christ. They appeared before the consistory of the church upon the same evening, say five years ago. Now five years have passed by. One of them may have grown far into the stature of Christ. He took seriously his vows to make diligent use of the means of grace; he was faithfully present under the preaching of the Word of God and faithfully received the blessing of the sacrament. Perhaps he is a Sunday School teacher now, or a deacon in the church. Perhaps he is a pillar in the church, strong enough to support those who are weak. The other young man may be just where he was five years ago, a mere babe in the faith, a babe who must be carried along by others, because his own faith, if any, is so weak and juvenile that he is still unable to stand alone.

This is why talk of spiritual birthdays and spiritual age is meaningless as many use these terms. If we were to speak in terms which are commonly employed by some, we would say that both of these men are five years of age spiritually. To make such a statement would be to demonstrate a complete lack of spiritual discernment. These two men are years apart spiritually. They may be the same age chronologically, the same age mentally and emotionally; they made their confessions of faith on the same evening five years ago, but today they are years apart spiritually.

We have said that sanctification is achieved by a conscious striving for growth in the Christian life. If anyone should ask, "What must I do? What steps must I take in order that I may grow in the faith and in the likeness of Christ?" I would reply, "Hear the word of Paul who said, 'work out your own salvation with fear and trembling: For it is God which worketh in you both to will and to do of his good pleasure.' " (Phil. 2:12-13). Notice that Paul is speaking to the man in whom God is already at work. The Spirit of God has touched this man's heart; he has been born again into newness of life; he has repented of his sin and placed faith in Christ as his Savior. Now, therefore, ". . . work out your own salvation in fear and trembling." This is of such vast import that Paul added "in fear and trembling." If you should ask further, "But how shall I work it out?" The answers are clear and specific.

The Bible sets forth several "means of grace" which are means to growth in The Faith. The first and foremost of these is the preaching of the Word of God. Perhaps you wonder why your pastor is constantly imploring you to be more faithful and consistent in your attendance upon the worship services of the church. Perhaps you say to yourself, "Is this one of the idiosyncracies of the preacher? Is this just a peculiarity on his part?" Not at all. One of the foremost principles of the new life is; If you would grow in the Christian life, you must come under the preaching of the Word of God, faithfully, consistently, unfailingly, and everlastingly. This is the principal means of grace set forth in the Word of God. It precedes every other; it is foundational to every other. The soul that would grow must come under the preaching of the Word.

Secondly, the soul that would grow must receive the grace which is communicated through the sacraments. Surely we need not repeat here that the grace which man may receive through the sacraments is not mechanically communicated. He who would be blessed by the sacraments must come in the proper attitude of mind and heart, that is, in true repentance and real faith. When a man does so come, the sacraments become to him a second means of grace, whereby his life is blessed unto growth into the stature of Christ. This is the second of the two principal means of grace, the faithful and right use of the sacraments.

There are also other means of grace. I shall mention but

one of the more important of these. This is the so-called "family altar," worship in the home, the reading of the Word of God, and prayer as the family is gathered together. Your home must become a sanctuary in which God is worshipped daily and every day, if you are to grow in the Christian life.

There is no other way. Take these means of grace away and growth in the Christian life is, humanly speaking, an impossibility. One day God will call me to account for your souls; therefore, permit me to say this to you in all kindness, "If the extent of your Christian life and experience consists in attending an occasional morning worship service, it is incredible that you should grow and develop in the Christian faith and life." Will you hear that? For your soul's sake, will you believe it? You cannot work out your salvation in that way. You can do so, only if you take advantage of every means of grace. How I would that I might implant this truth in your souls; how I would that I might make you see it and believe it; there is no other way to work out your salvation.

Believe me, I know the problem for many of you. It is like that of the sick man who has lost his appetite. He needs to eat; he needs nourishment to regain his health and strength, but at the very time that he needs nourishment most, he has no desire for food. This is the problem for many of you. You have no appetite for spiritual nourishment; you have no desire to partake of spiritual things; therefore, you continue in your weak and run-down spiritual condition. If you are wise, however, you will do what the doctor sometimes advises the sick man to do, that is, to compel himself to eat, even when he has no desire for food. If he will do this, he will often regain his health and strength; his appetite will return; he begins to enjoy the food which once he found it necessary to compel himself to eat.

Will you take this prescription for your illness? I know that some have no desire for spiritual nourishment. Some appear to have lost what ever appetite they may once have had for spiritual things. For the sake of your soul, therefore, compel yourself to do exactly what you do not feel like doing, compel yourself to come under the preaching of the Word, compel yourself to faithfully seek the blessing of the sacrament; conduct worship in your home, even though you must drive yourself to do it, even though other things must be set aside, even though it seems an inconvenience and a nuisance.

Do you know what will happen? If God be in you, I can promise you two things. First, you will grow in the faith; your life will become more and more patterned after the life of Christ. Second, you will gain a new appetite for the things of God. The day will come when you will feel as though the whole day had been lost, if you have not worshipped God in your home that day. The time will come when you will feel as if the whole week were lost, if you have not worshipped in the church on the Lord's Day. For the present, however, if you are in any wise serious about the matter of your salvation, then you must compel yourself to do the very things you have no desire to do.

Meantime I must point out to you, even as does the Word of God, if you claim to be a Christian, a follower of Jesus Christ, but you have gone along now for weeks, for months, for years perhaps, without coming one step closer to Christ than you were before, your life represents a paradox, an anomaly. There is no such thing, really, as a Christian who does not grow.

Do you remember the circus posters of years ago? An "after-show" followed the circus itself. Sometimes the "after-show" consisted of a troup of midgets, little people of mature years, people who were thirty, forty, fifty years of age, but whose stature was that of a ten year old child. A midget may constitute an attraction for a circus audience. Have you considered, however, what a burden it would be in real life to have people stare at you wherever you go, looking down at you, *the things which God hath prepared for them that love him.*

But God hath revealed them unto us by his Spirit: for the Spirit searcheth all things, yea, the deep things of God.

For what man knoweth the things of a man, save the spirit of man which is in him? even so the things of God knoweth no man, but the Spirit of God.

Now we have received, not the spirit of the world, but the spirit which is of God; that we might know the things that are freely given to us of God.

Which things also we speak, not in the words which man's wisdom teacheth, but which the Holy Ghost teacheth; comparing spiritual things with spiritual.

But the natural man receiveth not the things of the Spirit of God: for they are foolishness unto him: neither can he know them, because they are spiritually discerned.

But he that is spiritual judgeth all things, yet he himself is judged of no man.

For who hath known the mind of the Lord, that he may instruct him? But we have the mind of Christ.
—I Corinthians 2:1-16

The final step in the redemption of man is called "glorification." Perhaps I should say, more correctly, that glorification consists in a series of steps whereby man is fitted for life in the presence of God, and this series of steps are the final ones in the preparation of man for eternal life in the Kingdom of Heaven. Thus, a study of "glorification" takes one beyond the circumference of this world. It is not only futuristic in content, but it takes one beyond the scope of time into the realm of the eternal. Glorification is closely related to the ultimate realization of "eternal life."

This fact is suggested by that article of the Apostle's Creed in which we confess, "I believe in the life everlasting," and by the interpretation which the catechism places upon that article. The catechism asks, "What comfort takest thou from the article of life everlasting?" And it answers, "That since I now feel in my heart the beginning of eternal joy, after this life I shall inherit perfect salvation, which eye hath not seen, nor ear heard, neither hath it entered into the heart of man to conceive, and to praise God therein forever." (Lord's Day XXII, Q. 58).

You will have recognized that the answer of the catechism is taken largely, word for word, from the pages of the New Testament. This is all that the catechism seeks to do at any point, to set before us, in the plainest possible way, the teachings of the Bible. In this instance the words which are quoted are those of Paul who tells us that the "eye hath not seen, ear hath not heard, neither hath it entered into the heart of man to conceive of the things which God hath prepared for them that love Him."

Paul also referred to this fact in the midst of the many afflictions which he suffered as an apostle of the Lord Jesus Christ when he said, "I reckon that the sufferings of this present time are not worthy to be compared to the glory which shall be revealed in us" (Rom. 8:18). How many of God's people have found comfort and consolation in the midst of illness, suffering, pain, and even at death's door, remembering the words of Paul, and the Spirit of God testifying to their hearts that Paul spoke truly when he wrote, "I reckon that the sufferings of this present time are not worthy to be compared with the glory that shall be revealed in us."

This comfort derives from the fact that when God has made of us a new creation, He will not see that new creation destroyed. It derives from the fact that once He has begun a work of grace in us, He will not see that work disrupted or nullified. He will, rather, bring our redemption to a triumphant conclusion. Thus the Scriptures set before us a "golden chain" of events which are inter-related with each other in God's design for the accomplishment of our redemption. This is another aspect of the statement of Paul, ". . . whom He did predestinate, them He also called: and whom He called, them He also justified: and whom He justified, them He also glorified" (Rom. 8:30).

Consider these words as setting forth a golden chain of events which stretches from eternity to eternity, from the counsels of God before the worlds were framed to the ultimate realization of the kingdom of heaven. We become conscious of the working of God in our lives at the point of conversion. From this point of perspective we may look backward to our election in the Counsels of God before the worlds were framed and forward to our ultimate glorification in the kingdom of heaven. Because we have been called to repentance and faith, and because we have responded to the gracious invitation from God, we can know that we have been predestinated unto eternal life. This is the testimony of the Spirit to our hearts. Again, because we have been called of God, and have responded to that gracious invitation in repentance and faith, we know that He has also justified us, and therefore, we can know, with a faith born of God in our hearts, that He will bring the work, which He began in our calling and continued in our justification, to a triumphant conclusion in our glorification.

One fact we must have clearly before us however; it is the relationship between the present and the future. Only what we possess now, in this world and in this life, as a present reality, will we possess more perfectly and more completely in the life of the world to come. Only if we are joined to Christ here and now, and our union with Him is expressed in a true faith, even though imperfectly in the present life, will we enjoy that perfect relationship to Him which is set forth as the Christian Hope.

To this end I call two Biblical texts to your attention. The first comes from the pen of Paul as he wrote, "Our citizenship is in heaven" (Phil. 3:20 ASV). Note the tense of the verb. It is in the present tense, not the future. "Our citizenship *is* in heaven." If one is ever to hold citizenship in the Kingdom of Heaven, he must acquire it in this life and in this world. How, then, does one acquire citizenship in the heavenly kingdom? Paul answers this question too, for he writes that whereas once we were "aliens to the commonwealth of Israel . . . now . . . [we] are made nigh by the blood by Christ" (Eph. 2:12-13). Christ purchased citizenship for his own by his death upon the cross. Our faith in Him and in what He has done for us is our assurance that we have citizenship in the heavenly kingdom. We have it here; we have it now; and this is our assurance, and our only assurance that we shall have it forever.

Even more helpful to our understanding, perhaps, is the second text, which is found in John's Gospel. There we read, "He that believeth on the Son hath everlasting life" (John 3:36). Again I must ask you to note the tense of the verb. Again the tense is present, not future. "He that believeth on the son *has* [not will have but presently has] everlasting life." If, therefore, any man is to receive everlasting life, he must do so, not in some other world, not at some future date; he must acquire it in this world and in this life.

What does this mean? It means, simply, that everlasting

life is a continum; it begins in this world and on this side of death; it continues through death and into the world which lies beyond death. We sometimes speak of "another life"; we all do it, but correctly and Biblically speaking, this is not correct. There is no other life which begins on the other side of death. Everlasting life must be acquired here and now, if it is to be acquired at all.

The hallmark of the new life, the continuing life, the everlasting life, is faith in the Son of God and his redemptive work upon the cross, born out of our union with Him. When we are joined to Him, his life becomes our life, and this new life in us cannot die, anymore than God can die. Death cannot quench it; death cannot terminate it; death cannot put an end to our new life anymore than death can put an end to God. Eternal life is, therefore, a present reality for those who are joined to Christ in the bond of which our faith is the seal.

Now Paul tells us further that when we first receive this new life, we are as "babes," babes in the faith, spiritual babes. This situation is comparable to that of the new born babe in physical life. The infant child must be nourished and fed, if he is to grow and develop. So must the new spiritual life within us. This new spiritual life grows and develops on the Word of God, through the proper use of the sacraments, through prayer, through Christian experience and service. In every true Christian this growth and development continues for as long as he remains in this world.

Then one day death occurs. Contrary to the opinion of the secular world, death is not a tragedy, but the first step in the glorification of the believer. Should I say that again? Death is the first step in the glorification of the believer.

Why is this the case? For two reasons. First, for as long as we remain in this world, we have two natures within us, the new nature born of water and the Spirit, the new spiritual nature which shall never die, but we also have within us the corrupt nature of the natural man. That is why Paul speaks of his own battle against what he calls the "old man." This

GLORIFICATION: COMPLETE REDEMPTION

is common human experience among Christians, isn't it? Many of the temptations which beset us are, not on the outside but within; they arise out of ourselves. This is the old sinful nature continuing to assert itself.

Now we understand that this old nature was crucified with Christ, but just as crucifixion was a slow and agonizing death, so this old nature within us is slow to die, and it rises up in its death struggle from time to time and causes grave problems of sin in our lives. We can and we must do something about this problem which lies imbedded in our breasts. As we feed and nourish the new nature within us, as the new nature grows and develops, the old nature is mortified; its strength is diminished; the old nature decreases as the new nature increases within us.

Even so, the old nature is not finally dead, until the death of the body occurs. When physical death occurs, when the soul departs the body, it is the new nature, the new life, which is translated into the presence of God. The old, sinful nature dies; it cannot enter into the kingdom of heaven. Therefore, this internal enemy of our old nature, against which we have battled throughout our entire lives, is forever destroyed when the soul departs the body. The internal battle in man is over. The old nature, which has been a drag upon him all through his life in this world, is gone. He is freed from the old nature; he is a liberated man.

More than that, at the time of physical death, when the soul departs the body, the essential being, for the soul is the essence of man's being, is liberated, freed from the sin stricken body which has been a weight upon him all through the years. This is a blessed experience from two points of view. First, the body is presently the source of much temptation to us. The needs of the body are real needs. At no time does the Word of God declare to us that we are to deny the needs of the body. In our sinful condition, however, we often fail to distinguish between the needs of the body and the "lusts of the flesh." Perhaps no greater temptation faces the Christian in the materialistic age in which we live than the temptation to place our physical desires before our spiritual needs. Is not this the basic reason that men "rob God" of his tithes and offerings, the desire to obtain additional creature comforts, even at the expense of withholding from God what is justly his? Is not this the basic reason that men, and women too, often think themselves too busy to serve God more fully? Their business is created by an inordinate desire to gain more of the creature comforts of the world.

When the soul departs the body, this source of temptation ceases to exist. Not only the lusts of the flesh, but the very needs of the body will exist no more, neither shall we have any more need of fulfilling those physical requirements. The desire for creature comforts will cease to exist along with the body, as the dust returns to the earth from which it was taken, and the spirit returns unto God who gave it (cf. Eccles. 12:7).

The departure of the soul from the body will also constitute a blessed release in another sense. The human body, stricken by sin and the ravages of sin as it is, forms a weight upon man all through his life. I suppose that the afflicted and the elderly will appreciate this fact far more than the young and vigorous. There is a time in the lives of most when, being filled with the strength and vigor of youth, the body is viewed with pleasure, rather than as an encumbering weight. I say this is true for most, for even in youth, some are weighed down with the afflictions of the body. As people advance in years, however, this becomes more and more generally true. With the advance of age more diseases and impairments strike, and the body becomes more and more an encumbrance. Even in those few who live out their days in comparative physical health, the weaknesses and frailties become more and more apparent in the body and make it to be more and more of an encumbrance.

I scarcely need to speak to you of those instances in which the body becomes an instrument of torture. I have come into the homes and hospitals where your loved ones lay in agony and pain. I have suffered with you, for though I may know some of the biblical and theological answers to pain, I find it no less difficult to look upon human suffering than do you. Some people may grow hard and calloused, but I think that most of us are alike in this: we cringe at the sight of an animal in pain, not to mention another human. In these terrible instances, the body becomes an instrument of sheer torture, a prison-house of pain. What blessed release and relief, then, when the person is liberated, set free from the weight and pain of the body.

And this body must be left behind. It is not only a blessed relief but a necessity that the body be left behind. The physical body is marked and scarred by the sin of the race. Its weakness, its susceptibility to disease and pain, its vulnerability to death, are the ravages of sin in the human body. All this must be left behind. Neither sin nor the ravages of sin can enter into the kingdom of heaven. We are freed, both internally and externally, of all the ravages of sin when we depart this world and enter into the presence of God. Thus, death represents a long step toward our ultimate glorification.

This brings one to what is commonly called the "intermediate state." By the "intermediate state" we mean that state or condition upon which the soul enters as it departs the body, and in which it continues until body and soul are rejoined in the resurrection of the last day. Jesus referred to this state when he said to the repentant Thief upon the cross, "Today thou shalt be with me in Paradise." This means, simply, that he who has been joined to Christ in this world continues to be with Christ in the world that lies on the other side of death. With Christ; not in purgatory; not in the grave; not asleep; but with Christ around the throne of God, enjoying a conscious state of blessedness.

The "intermediate state" constitutes another phase in the glorification of the redeemed, both as individuals and as the Body of Christ. Why is this so? Because the joy of the individual and of the Body is made increasingly complete, only as other redeemed souls come to be with them in the estate of blessedness with Christ. This ought not to be too difficult to comprehend; we experience it in our daily family lives, if we are truly a family at all. Every member of the family wants for every other member all that he has for himself. The father of the family could not be happy in fine clothing, if his wife and children were in tatters. The mother of the family could not find happiness in a sumptuous feast, if her husband and children were hungry. And how many homes are overcast by a shadow, because a son or a daughter, perhaps grown, perhaps married, is living an unfortunate life or undergoing some painful experience.

So with the redeemed as they are gathered about the throne of God. As each new person passes through the experience of death, or should I say the doorway of death, as each new person is relieved of all the ravages of sin and enters into the blessed life, the joy of all those who are already present at the throne of God becomes increasingly full and complete. To be sure, the joy of those who are gathered about the throne of God will not be absolutely complete, until the last redeemed soul has entered into blessedness, and that is at least one of the reasons why God will not bring human history to its termination, nor the plan of redemption to its conclusion, until the last elect soul has been redeemed from sin.

The redeemed, in a very real sense, are also a family, you see. We sometimes speak of them as "the family of the redeemed." They are God's family. And when the last member of the family has come home, then the joy of the whole family, and the joy of each member of the family is made complete and full. Thus, the entry of God's people, one by one, into his presence is a further step in the glorification of all those who have entered into blessedness; their joy becomes the more full and complete, until at last the total number is in.

The next step in the glorification of the redeemed is the resurrection of the body in the last day. Man is an entity, both body and soul. While it is quite correct to say that the essence of man is his soul, and also correct to say that the person departs the body in physical death, yet, we must also observe that the body gives expression to the very essence of man, to the very image of God in man. And Christ died for the redemption of the whole man. We often speak about the salvation of the soul, and we do this to lay emphasis upon the essential spiritual nature of man, but at the same time, we realize that Christ died to redeem the whole man in body and soul.

We must have one point clearly before us. The resurrection of the body constitutes a reunion of body and soul. In the resurrection man does not receive a new body, in the sense of the resurrection body being totally unrelated to his original body. The body he receives is not divorced from the original body; the resurrection body is a glorification of the original or natural body. You say, "O, but it is a very different body that we will receive." So it is, and yet, it is to be identified with the old body. In essence it is the same body, now glorified. When one plants wheat, Paul tells us, it is wheat that comes forth, and when one plants corn, it is corn that comes forth; so each body will come forth having its own identity, related to the original body in much the same sense that the flower is related to the seed which was planted in the ground.

The fourth step in the glorification of the redeemed is the judgment. Now the judgment is often set forth as a thing to be feared, and so it ought to be by those who have lived upon this earth in disregard and defiance of God. How different for the redeemed! For them it is a time of vindication. O, this was meaningful to the apostles and the prophets in their terrible times of persecution; they looked forward with anticipation to that great day when their faith would be vindicated, and those who had cruelly persecuted them would meet their just judgment at last. It was equally meaningful to the Reformers in the terrible persecutions which accompanied the Reformation. They were accused of heresy and blasphemy and infamy, because they dared to believe that salvation is to be had in Christ alone. Their bodies were beaten and broken. They died in fiendish torment; their comfort lay in the knowledge that, in the last day, standing before the judgment bar of God, their faith would be vindicated, and their persecutors would meet a just judgment at last.

The catechism bears testimony to our forefathers' vital awareness of this fact, for it asks, "What comfort is it to thee that 'Christ shall come again to judge the quick and the dead'?" And it answers, "That in all my sorrows and persecutions, with uplifted head, I look for [Him] . . . to come as Judge from heaven, who shall cast all his and my enemies into everlasting condemnation, but shall translate me with all his chosen ones to Himself, into heavenly joys and glory." (Lord's Day XIX, Q. 52).

In the judgment, too, the redeemed shall receive the reward of their faith, their trials, their labors and their sorrows for the sake of Christ. Though we merit nothing from God, though we owe all things to God and to our Redeemer, yet God does not allow the faithful to go unrewarded. In that day every tear which has been shed in the name of Christ, every sacrifice which has been made in his service, every labor and trial which has been borne for the sake of his kingdom shall receive its reward. Thus, the judgment becomes the fourth step in the glorification of the redeemed.

The last step in the glorification of the redeemed is their entry into the "new heavens and the new earth." John provides the picture in his Revelation, and what a picture it is. John records, "I saw a new heaven and a new earth, for the first heaven and the first earth were passed away; and there was no more sea. And I, John, saw the holy city, new Jerusalem, coming down from God out of heaven, prepared as a bride adorned for her husband. And I heard a great voice out of heaven saying Behold, the tabernacle of God is with men, and He will dwell with them, and they shall be his people, and God Himself shall be with them and be their God. And God shall wipe all tears from their eyes; and there shall be no more death, neither sorrow, nor crying, neither shall there be any more pain: for the former things are passed away" (Rev. 21:1-4). Then is the glorification of the redeemed complete, when they have entered into the new heavens and the new earth.

Is not that a magnificent picture! At the same time I trust that you have not permitted it to obscure the crucial point in the whole matter. You see, the crucial point occurs at physical death. When the soul, the person, departs the body and this world, his destiny is forever fixed. Just as the redeemed go on into the presence of God, so the condemned are banished from the presence of God. Just as each new entry into blessedness adds to the joy of the redeemed, so does each new entry into the everlasting darkness contribute to the agony of those who dwell in banishment from God. Just as the resurrection of the body brings completion to the redemptive work of God in his people, so the resurrection body brings completion to the curse of those who die without Christ. Just as the judgment is a time of vindication and satisfaction to the redeemed, so is it a time of rejection and condemnation to those who have denied the authority of God in the world and rejected the redemption he has provided. Just as the redeemed enter into the full and complete joy of the new heavens and the new earth, so the lost enter into the utter desolation of eternal perdition.

Here and now the die is cast. Here and now you must enter upon eternal life or be forever banished from the presence of God. "He that believeth on the Son hath everlasting life, but he that believeth not is condemned already, in that he hath not believed on the only begotten Son of God. . . . And this is the judgment, that the Light is come into the world, and men preferred the darkness to the light, for their deeds were evil" (John 3:19, 36.) Ah, yes, and they that prefer the darkness shall have it; they shall have it for all eternity.

Hear, therefore, the invitation of Christ. Come confessing your sin; come in faith believing. Enter into life now, that you may live through all eternity.